PENGUIN HANDBOOKS

CHOCOLATE, CHOCOLATE, CHOCOLATE

Barbara Myers is the author of *Christmas Cookies and Candies*, *Christmas Entertaining*, *Great Dinner Parties*, *Woman's Day Old-Fashioned Desserts*, and *The Chinese Restaurant Cookbook*. She and her family live in Scarsdale, New York.

CHOCOLATE, CHOCOLATE, CHOCOLATE

Barbara Myers

PENGUIN BOOKS

Penguin Books Ltd, Harmondsworth,
Middlesex, England
Penguin Books, 40 West 23rd Street,
New York, New York 10010, U.S.A.
Penguin Books Australia Ltd, Ringwood,
Victoria, Australia
Penguin Books Canada Limited, 2801 John Street,
Markham, Ontario, Canada L3R 1B4
Penguin Books (N.Z.) Ltd, 182–190 Wairau Road,
Auckland 10, New Zealand

First published in the United States of America by
Rawson Associates 1983
First published in Canada by
McClelland and Stewart, Limited, 1983
Published in Penguin Books 1984

LIBRARY OF CONGRESS CATALOGING IN PUBLICATION DATA
Myers, Barbara.
Chocolate, chocolate, chocolate.
Reprint.   Originally published: New York: Rawson
Associates, c1983.
Includes index.
1. Cookery (Chocolate)   2. Desserts.   I. Title.
TX767.C5M93   1984   641.6'374   84-6343
ISBN 0 14 046.661 4

Printed in the United States of America by
R. R. Donnelley & Sons Company, Harrisonburg, Virginia
Set in Garamond

CONTENTS

CHOCOLATE,
CHOCOLATE,
CHOCOLATE

I

CHOCOLATE~FOOD OF THE GODS

The basis for all chocolate, and ultimately all delicious chocolate desserts, is the cocoa bean.

The bean comes from the seed pods of a tropical tree, the cacao tree, or the *Theobroma cacao,* "the food of the gods."

The cocoa pods, which look something like elongated acorn squash, are cut from the tree and split open. The seeds (or beans) inside—as many as twenty-five to fifty per pod—are scooped out along with the surrounding pulp, cured so .that they may be loosened from the pulp, and fermented to remove the bitter taste and let the essential oils develop. The beans are then dried and shipped to a processor.

Differences in quality and type of chocolate result from the varying treatments given to the cocoa beans during the processing when the manufacturer takes over.

In the factory the cocoa beans are first checked for quality, then carefully selected and blended—much the same way coffee beans are—for taste, texture, and aroma. They then go through several preliminary mechanical processes. First the beans are cleaned; then they are roasted to bring out the color and develop the "chocolate" flavor and aroma. This process also loosens the outer shell, which is removed, to reveal the meat (or nib) of the bean, from which the chocolate is made.

These nibs, which are more than half cocoa butter (a vegetable fat), are then processed by grinding. The grinding procedure melts the cocoa butter and leaves a thick, rich brown paste which is called chocolate liquor. In subsequent finer grindings, called conching, the paste is further refined to improve the quality.

When the liquor is poured into molds and is solidified, unsweetened (or bitter) chocolate is the result. Additional processing provides sweetened chocolate, milk chocolate, and cocoa.

In the making of unsweetened cocoa, the chocolate liquor is put into presses which remove about half the cocoa butter. The resulting cakelike residue is pulverized, then sifted to a fine cocoa powder.

To produce sweetened chocolate (bittersweet, semisweet, or sweet), sugar is added in varying amounts. Some of the cocoa butter is restored, vanilla flavoring is added, and more conching takes place. If milk is added, it becomes milk chocolate.

The quality of the sweetened chocolate is determined not only by the amounts of chocolate liquor, cocoa butter, and sugar used but also by how much more the chocolate is refined, or conched. The longer it is conched, the smoother and the less astringent the flavor of the chocolate becomes.

Variations in the processing—including blending of different beans—produce the distinctive flavor of each brand of chocolate on the market.

All chocolate that meets U.S. federal standards of identification is classified as real chocolate, and all real chocolate contains cocoa butter. Other chocolate products, which are usually made from cocoa, substitute vegetable oil for the cocoa butter and must be labeled "chocolate-flavored." They are not as chocolaty as real chocolate and therefore work less well in recipes.

A list of the different types of chocolate follows.

TYPES OF CHOCOLATE

UNSWEETENED CHOCOLATE

This is the purest of all cooking chocolate. The bitter flavor is intense and full-bodied since there are no additives. The chocolate is readily available in supermarkets, sold in 8-ounce packages, with individually wrapped squares of 1 ounce each. American brands (there are no foreign counterparts) are Baker, Hershey, and Wilbur.

Baker also produces a premelted unsweetened chocolate-flavored product in 1-ounce packets. It is a blend of cocoa and vegetable oil, not cocoa butter. For the best chocolate flavor use real chocolate instead.

UNSWEETENED COCOA POWDER

Cocoa powder is made from the dry portion of the chocolate liquor that remains after much of the cocoa butter has been removed. It is unsweetened. Sweetened cocoa products do exist; do not use them by mistake. Because it is widely available, Hershey's cocoa was used in the testing of the recipes in this book.

Dutch-process cocoa has been treated with an alkali to neutralize the natural acids. This gives it a darker color and makes it less bitter. This cocoa may be used successfully in any recipe unless baking powder or baking soda is called for. Natural cocoa and Dutch-processed cocoa differ in the amounts required. (Droste brand and Van Houten from the Netherlands are representative.)

Note: It is not advisable to substitute cocoa in a recipe that calls for unsweetened chocolate since the cocoa butter in the chocolate gives it a richer, more chocolaty flavor. In a pinch, however, substitute 3 level tablespoons of cocoa plus 1 tablespoon vegetable shortening for each 1 ounce of unsweetened chocolate.

SEMISWEET CHOCOLATE

The base is unsweetened chocolate, but semisweet chocolate contains more cocoa butter and is flavored with sugar and vanilla. There are many brands, some American, some imported; the quality varies, as does the flavor.

Baker is the domestic leader, but there are also Maillard and Kron. Among the preferred foreign chocolates are: Swiss bars, such as Tobler, Lindt, and Suchard; Perugina from Italy;

Feodora and Sarotti from Germany; and Van Houten from the Netherlands. Some of these manufacturers make an extra-bittersweet as well as a bittersweet chocolate.

Frequently price is the best indicator of quality in chocolate, and some of these brands are very expensive. Many chocolate lovers, however, feel that the difference in quality justifies the price.

Baker's semisweet chocolate is conveniently packaged in 1-ounce squares, eight to a package. The others are in bar form, usually in 3-ounce packages. They are sometimes available in the gourmet section of the supermarket, but are more often found in specialty food shops or at confectionaries.

Note: Any of these chocolates may be used interchangeably in any recipe calling for semisweet chocolate. See also "Semisweet Chocolate Morsels," which follows.

SEMISWEET CHOCOLATE MORSELS

These teardrop-shaped pieces of chocolate are variously called morsels, bits, or chips according to the manufacturer. The chocolate is semisweet in flavor and is sold in 6- and 12-ounce bags. A 6-ounce bag yields 1 cup; the 12-ounce yields 2 cups. Although these morsels are primarily intended for baking, when it is desirable for the chocolate to retain its shape, they may also be grated or melted as an acceptable substitute for other semisweet chocolate. (See "Grating Chocolate," page 9, and "Melting Chocolate," page 8.)

The most familiar brands are Nestlé and Hershey, but many supermarkets have their own brands. The only important caution is to be sure that the morsels are real chocolate, not merely chocolate-flavored.

DARK SWEET CHOCOLATE

Dark sweet chocolate, which is sweeter than semisweet chocolate, is available only in bar form. The most readily available and familiar is Baker's German's sweet chocolate, sold in 4-ounce bars. Other excellent brands include Hershey's special dark, Maillard Eagle sweet chocolate, and Goya sweet chocolate.

Note: This chocolate may be used with satisfactory results in any recipe that calls for semisweet chocolate.

MILK CHOCOLATE

This sweet chocolate has dried milk solids added to the chocolate formula with a blend of other ingredients. It is light in color and mild in flavor. The well-known Hershey bar and the Hershey milk chocolate morsels are readily available in supermarkets, as is the Nestlé bar. Other milk chocolate bars, such as those produced by Cadbury, Ghirardelli, or Sarotti (German) are less frequently available, but worth seeking.

Note: Milk chocolate should be used only in recipes that specifically call for it; do not substitute for dark sweet or semisweet chocolate.

WHITE CHOCOLATE

White chocolate is not chocolate at all; it is a blend of whole milk and sugar, cooked until it is condensed to a solid state. Sometimes cocoa butter is added to produce the chocolate flavor; if not, artificial flavor is added.

White chocolate is available in unwrapped bar form or in chunks at stores where fresh candies are sold. It is difficult to know whether or not cocoa butter is used, but the imported brand Tobler Narcisse does include cocoa butter. Tobler and Lindt also have bars that include nuts and additional flavorings. Unless you want to add these ingredients, do not use them instead of plain white chocolate.

STORING CHOCOLATE

Chocolate is best when stored in a cool, dry place at a temperature of about 68 to 78 degrees. At higher temperatures the chocolate is likely to develop a bloom, or grayish color, which results when the cocoa butter rises to the surface, where it remains. Should your chocolate produce a bloom, it is still usable as long as it remains firm and does not become crumbly. The flavor and color will return to normal when melted.

MELTING CHOCOLATE

The key to melting chocolate is gentle heat. It should be melted slowly and evenly. Chocolate melted at too high a temperature will scorch, turn bitter, and stiffen into an unusable mass. Stiffening will also occur if the cooking container is not completely dry since even a drop or two of moisture can cause the chocolate to seize.

The preferred ways to melt chocolate are over direct heat or in a double boiler. When using direct heat, make sure that the saucepan is heavy and that the heat is *very* low. When using a double boiler—whether it is a regular two-piece pan or a mixing bowl set over a saucepan—use *barely* simmering water in the lower container. *Be sure that the bottom of the upper container does not come in contact with the water.* When the quantity of chocolate to be melted is small, say, three ounces or less, use the direct heat method and a small saucepan for best results.

Regardless of which method you use, in order to melt the chocolate smoothly and evenly, cut it into small pieces. Use a dry wooden cutting board and a dry chef's knife. Once it is over the heat and begins to soften, the chocolate should be stirred frequently with a wooden spoon. When it is barely melted, remove the pan from the heat and stir the chocolate rapidly until it is smooth.

Unsweetened chocolate will melt to a runny liquid even without stirring, whereas sweetened chocolate tends to retain its shape longer. As sweetened chocolate warms, its appearance changes from dull to shiny, but it will not liquefy until it is stirred.

Note: Semisweet chocolate morsels have a higher viscosity (resistance to flow) than other semisweet chocolate. They will melt more easily if 1 tablespoon vegetable shortening is added for each six ounces.

Dark sweet chocolate, milk chocolate, and *especially* white chocolate must be used as soon as they have been melted. Unsweetened chocolate and semisweet chocolate should be cooled slightly but can be kept up to 15 minutes, depending on quantity.

Note: The guidelines given above are meant to apply when chocolate is melted alone. When liquids are added—milk, cream, water, liquor—the melting procedures vary. Details are specified in the individual recipes.

GRATING CHOCOLATE

The easiest way to grate chocolate is to use an electric food processor. Chop the chocolate into coarse pieces; then process it, using on/off turns, until it is reduced to powdery-fine to coarse granules. (Whole semisweet chocolate morsels may be used.)

Chocolate can also be grated with a hand-held grater placed in a large mixing bowl. Use a cold large piece (chunk, bar, or square) of chocolate and the coarse side of the grater.

In the absence of both food processor and grater, chop the chocolate fine on a wooden cutting board, using a chef's knife.

PREPARING CHOCOLATE CONFECTIONS

These confections are the epitome of chocolate desserts. They are either nearly all chocolate or are dipped into melted chocolate to make an attractive glaze.

For an appealing appearance—a muted glossy sheen—the following guidelines should be observed:

1. As in the melting of all chocolate, a gentle, low, even heat is required (see "Melting Chocolate," page 8). Often vegetable shortening or oil is added for melting to thin the chocolate for proper dipping and to maximize the sheen of the glaze.

While the chocolate is melting, it must be stirred constantly. Stirring tempers the chocolate and ensures quicker hardening (setting) and good color. It is especially important that the melted chocolate be removed from the heat immediately. If it becomes too hot, the chocolate will turn grayish and dull when it sets.

2. It is important not to attempt to prepare these chocolate confections on an exceedingly hot, humid day unless your kitchen is air-conditioned.

Excess heat or moisture, even drafts, will prevent the chocolate from setting properly. The chocolate should cool and set relatively quickly. Long and slow cooling can also turn the chocolate gray or may cause the uneven streaking or spotting that results when the cocoa butter separates and rises to the surface.

3. Once cooled, the chocolate confections should be stored in airtight containers in a cool, dry place. They may be refrigerated or frozen, as long as they are securely wrapped.

When the confections are refrigerated or frozen, allow them to come to room temperature before you unwrap them. If you do not, they will "sweat," and the moisture will cause them to turn gray and to lose their sheen.

Note: Do not expect these confections to have the high gloss of commercial chocolates. For this, a different type of chocolate is used and extra expertise is required. At perfection the chocolate will have a dull satin gloss, which is equally appealing.

II

CHOCOLATE AND OTHER GARNISHES

When desserts are given decorations of contrasting color or texture, their appearance is enhanced and they become more tempting than when they are unadorned. Some garnishes are prepared simply; others are more difficult. Following are some of each, the use of which is suggested in several recipes throughout the book. Their use need not be limited to these recipes; many can be used interchangeably or added where no garnish is called for.

CHOCOLATE SCROLLS

Chocolate scrolls are easy to make and provide an attractive garnish for any appropriate dessert. They can be used in quantity to cover the top of a dessert but are also effective when a few perfect scrolls are placed on an individual serving.

To make the scrolls, 1-ounce squares of semisweet chocolate are required. Allow a square to stand in a warm place long enough so that it feels slightly warm to the touch (an unlit gas oven is ideal). Draw a vegetable peeler carefully across the large, flat side. The chocolate should come off in long, thin curls; if it splinters, the chocolate is not sufficiently warmed. Do this over a large plate. Let the scrolls stand for a few minutes until they have hardened enough to be handled (or briefly refrigerate them). Using a metal spatula, carefully transfer them to the top of the dessert to be garnished.

Note: Because these scrolls are fragile, they should not be made in advance and stored; excess handling will cause them to break up. Also, do not expect these scrolls to be in perfect cylinders; they will be uneven in shape and size.

CHOCOLATE SHAVINGS

This simple garnish is also made with a vegetable peeler. Although not as attractive as scrolls, shavings have certain advantages. Any type of chocolate may be used. The chocolate can be used without warming, and the "splinters" of chocolate are applied directly to the dessert.

To prepare, hold a piece of chocolate (square, bar, or chunk) directly over the dessert to be garnished. Scrape with a vegetable peeler, letting the thin shavings fall where you want them.

CHOCOLATE LACE

This is a simple but highly effective garnish. It is merely melted chocolate drizzled in a thin lacelike pattern over the top of a dessert, such as a pale-colored mousse or a pie or cake with a whipped cream topping.

For best results use part unsweetened chocolate so that the chocolate is thin. One ounce of semisweet chocolate melted with 1/2 ounce unsweetened chocolate will be sufficient to cover the top of a dessert that serves 6 to 8. Chop the chocolate into coarse pieces; place them in a small heavy saucepan, and set the pan over very low heat. Stir until the chocolate is melted and smooth; remove from the heat. Using a teaspoon, drizzle the chocolate in a thin stream, swirling it over the dessert so that it forms a lacy design. Refrigerate the dessert until the chocolate lace is set, about 5 minutes, or longer if preferred.

CHOCOLATE SPRINKLES

This is a commercially produced garnish, and available in most supermarkets. Although they have little flavor, these tiny elongated confections are useful in decorating desserts whenever a token garnish is desired.

CHOCOLATE DIPPED STRAWBERRIES

These beauties can be served alone as dessert, with dessert, or as a garnish.

> *26 to 30 large fresh strawberries*
> *4 ounces semisweet chocolate, chopped into coarse pieces*
> *1 tablespoon vegetable oil*

1. Use only berries with fresh-looking green caps and without blemishes or nicks (which could leak moisture after the fruits have been dipped). You will need to purchase at least a quart of berries to produce enough perfect ones of similar size. Do not rinse the berries; they must be perfectly dry. If necessary, clean them by brushing with a soft brush.

2. Line a cookie sheet with wax paper; set aside.

3. Combine the chocolate and oil in the top of a small double boiler, and set it over barely simmering water (or use a small mixing bowl set over a saucepan). Melt the chocolate, stirring constantly, until it is smooth and satiny. (The stirring "tempers" the chocolate and ensures good color and quicker hardening after the berries have been dipped.) Immediately remove the pan from the water; overcooking will turn the chocolate gray and dull when hardened.

4. Holding a berry by the cap (hull), dip it into the chocolate, turning it so that about two-thirds are coated and just a little of the red berry shows at the top. Allow the excess chocolate to drip back into the pan. Lay the berry on its side on the baking sheet. If too much excess chocolate drips onto the paper, stir the melted chocolate to cool slightly; then repeat with the remaining berries.

5. Allow the coated strawberries to stand at room temperature until the chocolate hardens; at this point they may be easily lifted off the paper.

Note: If the day is exceedingly hot, humid, or rainy, the chocolate may not set quickly; place briefly, about 10 minutes, in the refrigerator. However, do not store the coated berries in the refrigerator; this will cause the coating to "sweat" when returned to room temperature, and it will turn gray and lose its sheen.

6. Use the dipped strawberries within a few hours of coating—12 hours at the most—because they are perishable.

MAKES 26 TO 30 COATED BERRIES OR 4 DESSERT SERVINGS.

CHOCOLATE DIPPED ORANGE SEGMENTS

The procedure here is the same as for dipping strawberries. Select a variety of orange which is seedless and is easily peeled and pulled into sections, such as the navel, Tangelo, Jaffa, or Clementine.

> *3 to 4 small or medium-size seedless oranges*
> *4 ounces semisweet chocolate, chopped into coarse pieces*
> *1 tablespoon vegetable oil*

1. Using your fingertips, carefully peel the oranges, then gently separate into sections. Dry briefly on paper towel.

Note: Segments with small perforations in the membrane may be used; unlike strawberries they do not leak moisture after being dipped and enclosed in the chocolate coating.

2. Line a cookie sheet with wax paper; set aside.

3. Combine the chocolate and oil in the top of a small double boiler and set it over barely simmering water. (Or use a small mixing bowl set over a saucepan.) Melt the chocolate, stirring constantly, until it is smooth and satiny. (The stirring "tempers" the chocolate and ensures good color and quicker hardening after the orange segments have been dipped.) Immediately remove the pan from the water; overcooking will turn the chocolate gray and dull when hardened.

4. Holding one end of an orange segment, dip it into the melted chocolate, turning it so that about two-thirds is coated. Allow the excess chocolate to drip back into the pan. Place the segment curved-side down on the wax paper. If too much chocolate drips onto the paper, stir the melted chocolate to cool slightly, then proceed with the remaining orange sections.

5. When all of the sections have been coated, place briefly in the refrigerator to harden the chocolate, about 10 minutes. Return to room temperature until ready to serve.

6. For best quality serve the dipped orange segments within a few hours, as the exposed membrane surrounding the

juicy flesh tends to dry rapidly and will slightly toughen and eventually become brittle the longer it is exposed to air. However, the orange sections are still delicious when served a day or two after dipping.

MAKES ABOUT 30 COATED ORANGE SECTIONS.

CANDIED ORANGE OR LEMON PEEL

An appropriate garnish for any dessert made with citrus fruit. These candied julienne strips of peel should be used sparingly as a token garnish. Two or three atop a single serving is sufficient.

> *2 large thick-skinned oranges or 4 lemons*
> *6 tablespoons sugar*
> *1/4 cup water*

1. Using a vegetable peeler, remove the zest (none of the white) from the oranges or lemons in strips as wide as possible. Cut into thin, julienne (about 1/16-inch) strips, discarding the ragged edges.

2. Drop the peels into a small saucepan half-filled with boiling water; cook for 5 minutes. (This will remove some of the bitterness.) Remove from the heat, and drain in a wire sieve; then pat dry with paper toweling.

3. Combine the sugar and the water in the same saucepan; cook over low heat until the sugar is melted, occasionally swirling the pan gently.

4. Stir the orange or lemon peel into the syrup; then cook without stirring for about 30 minutes, or until the peel is glazed and candied. Pour the contents of the pan into a wire sieve to drain off the excess syrup.

5. Using a two-tined kitchen fork, place the peels on a cooling rack, separating them as best you can. As they begin to dry, continue to separate them so that they are in individual strips. Do not attempt to straighten them; they are more attractive when slightly curled. Allow the peels to dry completely. Store in an airtight container. They will keep well for weeks at room temperature.

MAKES ABOUT 1/2 CUP.

ALMOND PRALINE

Chopped coarse to be sprinkled over ice cream or used as a garnish on whipped cream toppings.

1 cup unblanched almonds
1 cup sugar
1/4 cup water
1/8 teaspoon cream of tartar

1. Scatter the almonds in a large, ungreased baking pan, one large enough so that the nuts are not layered. Bake in a preheated 350-degree oven for 10 to 15 minutes, stirring frequently so that they roast evenly. The skins should have darkened slightly, and you should detect the faint aroma of toasted nuts. (Remove one to test; when cut, the inside should look slightly darkened, barely toasted.) Remove from the oven, and set aside in the pan to cool.

2. Combine the sugar, water, and cream of tartar in a 1-quart heavy saucepan, stirring gently just to combine. Then cook over medium heat, without stirring, for about 5 minutes, or until the sugar is melted and turns amber. (Do not allow it to become too dark, or it will be bitter.)

3. Remove the caramelized sugar from the heat and immediately stir in the toasted nuts. Then return the pan to the heat, and stir until the nuts are well coated.

4. Pour onto a lightly oiled piece of foil (at least 12 inches square), which has been placed on a countertop. With the back of a spoon spread evenly and as quickly as possible because the syrup will begin to harden almost immediately. Allow to cool until hardened, at least 15 minutes; then break into irregular pieces.

5. Transfer the praline to a chopping board, and chop it into small, coarse pieces, about 1/8 to 1/4 inch in size. Store in an airtight container at room temperature. It will keep well for at least several weeks.

MAKES 2 CUPS.

ABOUT ALMONDS, HAZELNUTS, AND OTHER NUTS

Unlike walnuts and pecans, almonds and hazelnuts have thin skins, which are generally removed before using. This process is called blanching.

TO BLANCH ALMONDS

Cover the nuts with boiling water; let them stand for no longer than 3 minutes; then drain them. Slip off the skins by pinching each almond between your thumb and forefinger. Dry the nuts on paper toweling. Then place in a shallow baking pan, and bake in a preheated oven at 200 degrees for about 30 minutes to dry thoroughly. (Do not allow them to darken.)

TO BLANCH AND TOAST HAZELNUTS

These nuts have loose skins, which are removed by toasting. Place in one layer in a shallow baking pan. Bake on the lower rack in a preheated 350-degree oven for about 10 minutes, shaking the pan occasionally to toast the nuts evenly. When the skins are blistered and brittle, remove the nuts from the oven. Cool slightly; then place in a cloth towel, and rub lightly to remove most of the skins. Use as is, or use your fingertips to remove any remaining skin.

TO TOAST ALMONDS

For a small quantity, place whole blanched almonds in one layer in a dry, heavy skillet. Stir over low heat until they turn color. Do not overbrown; they will continue to darken as they cool. For a larger amount, place almonds in a shallow baking pan, and bake in a preheated oven at 350 degrees for about 10 to 15 minutes, shaking occasionally to toast evenly. They should emerge an even, light, and toasty brown.

Note: Thin-sliced almonds or the oblong-shaped slivered almonds may be used. Watch the toasting carefully.

TO GRIND NUTS

Many recipes call for ground nuts as a replacement for part or all of the flour. When they are ground, they should be light and fluffy and have a powdery quality. Nuts must be dry to be ground properly (see above: "To Blanch Almonds").

Use a nut grinder, a food processor, or a blender. A meat grinder will turn the nuts oily. A nut grinder or food processor is easier to use; a blender takes longer because only 1/2 cup can be ground at one time.

When using a food processor, process in short on/off turns to ensure that the heat generated by the speed of the blade does not draw out the oil of the nuts and make them pasty. To measure ground nuts, spoon them lightly into a measuring cup.

III

LAYER CAKES, LOAF CAKES, AND CUPCAKES

BUTTERMILK CHOCOLATE LAYER CAKE
SOUR CREAM CHOCOLATE CAKE
NOUGATINE CAKE
DOUBLE CHOCOLATE MALTED MILK CAKE
KENTUCKY BLUEGRASS FUDGE CAKE
BROWN SUGAR CHOCOLATE CAKE
PEANUT BUTTER CHOCOLATE CAKE
MISSISSIPPI MUD CAKE
SOUTHERN CHOCOLATE SHEET CAKE
SELF-ICED COCOA CAKE
DOUBLE CHOCOLATE CUPCAKES
CHOCOLATE TOWN SYRUP CUPCAKES
CHOCOLATE CREAM CHEESE CUPCAKES

BUTTERMILK CHOCOLATE LAYER CAKE

This is a dark two-layer cake filled with strawberry jam and frosted with an ivory-colored buttercream. The cake is rich and fragile, so care must be taken in handling it. It keeps well.

1/2 cup unsweetened cocoa powder
1 teaspoon baking soda
1/2 cup boiling water
1/2 cup vegetable shortening
2 cups sugar
2 eggs, at room temperature
1 teaspoon vanilla extract
2 cups sifted cake flour
1 teaspoon baking powder
1/2 teaspoon salt
1 cup buttermilk
Buttercream Frosting (recipe follows)
1/4 cup strawberry jam

1. Generously grease and flour two 9-inch-round layer cake pans. Preheat the oven to 350 degrees.

2. In a small bowl combine the cocoa and baking soda. Gradually add the boiling water, and stir until smooth. Set aside while preparing the remaining ingredients.

3. In the large bowl of an electric mixer cream the shortening with the sugar. Add the eggs, one at a time, beating until smooth after each addition. Beat in first the vanilla, then the cocoa mixture.

4. Sift the flour with the baking powder and salt. On low speed add the flour to the egg mixture alternately with the buttermilk, adding the flour in three additions, the buttermilk in two. Beat only until smooth after each addition.

5. Pour the batter into the prepared pans. Shake to level slightly. Bake for 30 minutes, or until the tops barely leave an

imprint when lightly touched. Do not overbake, or the layers
will be dry.

6. Cool the layers on racks for 15 minutes before turning
out. Invert so that they cool right side up.

7. Prepare the frosting. Then place one layer upside down
on a cake plate. Beat the jam lightly with a fork, adding a few
drops of hot water if necessary to produce a spreading consistency. Spread the jam over the top of the cake layer. Cover with
the second layer right side up; then spread the top and sides
with the frosting.

MAKES 10 TO 12 SERVINGS.

BUTTERCREAM FROSTING

1/4 cup (1/2 stick) unsalted butter, softened
2 egg yolks, at room temperature
1/4 teaspoon salt
1 teaspoon vanilla extract
3 1/2 cups sifted confectioners' sugar
About 1/4 cup milk

Cream the butter with the egg yolks, salt, and vanilla. Stir
in 1 cup of the sugar and 3 tablespoons of the milk. Add the
remaining sugar and beat until smooth. Add the remaining
milk, a teaspoonful at a time, as needed, beating until the
frosting holds its shape and is stiff enough to spread.

SOUR CREAM CHOCOLATE CAKE

*Three luscious ivory-colored layers filled and iced with a sour cream
chocolate frosting that gives the cake a piquant tinge.*

> 2 3/4 cups sifted cake flour
> 3 teaspoons baking powder
> 1 teaspoon baking soda
> 3/4 teaspoon salt
> 3/4 cup (1 1/2 sticks) unsalted butter, softened
> 1 1/2 cups sugar
> 4 egg whites, at room temperature
> 1 cup dairy sour cream
> 1/2 cup milk
> 1 teaspoon vanilla extract
> Sour Cream Chocolate Frosting (recipe follows)

1. Grease and flour three 8-inch-round layer cake pans.
Preheat the oven to 350 degrees.

2. Sift the flour with the baking powder, baking soda,
and salt several times until the mixture is well blended.

3. In the bowl of an electric mixer beat the butter until
creamy. Gradually add 1 cup of sugar, and continue beating
until the mixture is very, very smooth.

4. In a separate mixing bowl beat the egg whites until
they form soft peaks; then gradually beat in the remaining 1/2
cup sugar. Continue beating until the mixture forms a satiny-
smooth meringue that will stand in stiff peaks.

5. Place the sour cream in a small bowl. Gradually blend
in first the milk, then the vanilla.

6. Using a rubber spatula, stir about one-fourth of the
flour mixture into the creamed butter and sugar; add one-third
of the sour cream mixture. Repeat the additions, using the same
proportions, ending with the flour. (Use a rapid stirring action
to blend, but do not beat.)

7. Gently fold in the meringue mixture. Divide the batter equally among the prepared pans. Bake for about 25 minutes, or until the tops spring lightly back with a touch. Cool for about 5 minutes on racks; then turn out to cool completely.

8. Prepare the frosting. Spread between the layers and on the tops and sides. It should be spread smoothly and evenly. Refrigerate for at least 2 hours before serving.

MAKES 10 OR MORE SERVINGS.

SOUR CREAM CHOCOLATE FROSTING

12 ounces semisweet chocolate, chopped into coarse pieces
1 cup dairy sour cream
1/4 teaspoon salt
1 teaspoon vanilla extract
1 tablespoon rum or cognac

Melt the chocolate in the top of a double boiler set over barely simmering water. When it is partially melted, remove it from the water, and stir until smooth; allow it to cool. Then beat in the sour cream, followed by the salt, vanilla, and rum. Continue beating until spreadable.

NOUGATINE CAKE

A velvety-textured two-layer cake made with honey and just a hint of chocolate to flavor and color it lightly. A fluffy egg white frosting is used to frost the cake, part of which is combined with toasted almonds and glacéed cherries for the filling.

1/2 cup (3 ounces) semisweet chocolate morsels
1/2 cup boiling water
1 3/4 cups sifted cake flour
1 cup sugar
3/4 teaspoon salt
1/2 teaspoon baking powder
3/4 teaspoon baking soda
1/2 cup vegetable shortening
1/2 cup honey
1/3 cup buttermilk
1 teaspoon vanilla extract
2 eggs, at room temperature
Nougatine Frosting (recipe follows)
Chopped toasted almonds (page 20), optional garnish
Red and green candied cherries, optional garnish

1. Grease and flour two 9-inch-round layer cake pans. Preheat the oven to 350 degrees.
2. Pour the chocolate morsels into the large bowl of an electric mixer. Gradually add the boiling water, stirring until the chocolate is melted and blended. Set aside to cool.
3. Sift the flour, sugar, salt, baking powder, and baking soda over the melted chocolate. Add the shortening, honey, buttermilk, and vanilla. Beat for 2 minutes at medium speed. Scrape the bowl and beaters.
4. Add the eggs, and beat as before for 2 minutes. Again scrape the bowl; then stir the mixture lightly if necessary to be certain it is well blended.

5. Divide the batter evenly between the prepared pans, and bake for about 30 to 35 minutes, or until the centers test done with a wooden pick and the cake draws slightly away from the sides of the pans. Cool on racks for about 10 minutes; then turn out and cool completely.

6. Prepare the nougatine frosting as directed.

7. To assemble, place one layer on a cake plate and spread it with the reserved frosting that contains the almonds and cherries. Place the second layer on top; then frost the top and sides with the remaining frosting, spreading it smoothly or pulling it up in decorative points.

8. If desired, decorate the top of the cake with a "wreath" of chopped almonds and bits of red and green cherries. If this garnish is used, the top of the cake should be smoothly covered with the frosting.

Note: It is necessary to fill and frost the cake the day it is to be served. The cake layers, however, may be made a day in advance or frozen.

MAKES 12 SERVINGS.

NOUGATINE FROSTING

2 egg whites, at room temperature
1 1/2 cups sugar
1/4 cup water
2 tablespoons honey
2 tablespoons light corn syrup
1/4 teaspoon cream of tartar
1/8 teaspoon salt
1/2 teaspoon vanilla extract
1/2 cup coarse-chopped toasted, blanched almonds
2 tablespoons candied red cherries, cut into small pieces

1. Combine the egg whites, sugar, water, honey, corn syrup, cream of tartar, and salt in the top of a double boiler, and mix well. Place over rapidly boiling water and beat with an electric mixer at high speed for about 5 minutes, or until the mixture holds a peak when the beaters are withdrawn. (You may use a rotary beater, but the time will be longer, at least 7 minutes.)

2. Remove the pan from the water, add the vanilla, and continue beating until the mixture is thick enough to spread.

3. Remove about one-third of the mixture to a separate bowl, and fold in the almonds and cherries. Fill and frost the cake immediately.

DOUBLE CHOCOLATE MALTED MILK CAKE

An unusual two-layer cake with cocoa and malted milk powder used in both the cake and the soft and luscious chocolate frosting.

1/2 cup (1 stick) unsalted butter, softened
1 1/4 cups sugar
1/4 cup malted milk powder (natural, not cocoa-flavored)
3 eggs, at room temperature
2 cups sifted cake flour
1/2 cup unsweetened cocoa powder
2 1/2 teaspoons baking powder
1 teaspoon salt
3/4 cup milk
Chocolate Malt Frosting (recipe follows)

1. Preheat the oven to 350 degrees. Grease and flour two 9-inch layer cake pans.

2. In a large mixing bowl with electric beaters, cream the butter until light. Gradually beat in first the sugar, then the malted milk powder. Beat in the eggs, one at a time, beating well after each addition.

3. Sift together the flour, cocoa, baking powder, and salt. Add to the creamed mixture alternately with the milk, beating just until smooth after each addition.

4. Turn the batter into the prepared pans, dividing it evenly and spreading it to the sides. Bake for about 25 to 30 minutes, or until the centers spring back when lightly touched. Cool in the pans on a rack for 10 minutes; then turn out and cool completely.

5. Prepare the frosting. Spread it generously between the layers and on the top and sides. Allow the frosted cake to stand at room temperature to set the frosting; it will remain soft and creamy.

MAKES 12 SERVINGS.

CHOCOLATE MALT FROSTING

5 tablespoons unsalted butter, softened
1/2 teaspoon salt
1 1/2 tablespoons malted milk powder
1 teaspoon vanilla extract
2/3 cup unsweetened cocoa powder, sifted
1 cup heavy cream
3 cups confectioners' sugar, sifted

With an electric mixer set on low, thoroughly cream the butter, salt, malted milk powder, vanilla, and cocoa. Add the cream and sugar alternately, beating at medium speed until the mixture is very smooth and light and has a spreading consistency.

Note: This recipe makes a generous amount; use lavishly. It is easy to work with and stays soft and creamy.

KENTUCKY BLUEGRASS FUDGE CAKE

An old-time favorite two-layer cake calling for bourbon and pecans in both batter and frosting. It is moist and fudgy and therefore keeps well. In fact, this cake seems to taste better if it is made at least a day in advance.

> *1/2 cup (1 stick) unsalted butter, softened*
> *2 cups sugar*
> *4 ounces unsweetened chocolate, melted and cooled*
> *2 eggs, at room temperature*
> *1 teaspoon vanilla extract*
> *2 tablespoons bourbon*
> *2 cups sifted cake flour*
> *2 teaspoons baking powder*
> *1/2 teaspoon salt*
> *1 1/2 cups less 2 tablespoons milk*
> *1 cup fine-chopped pecans or black walnuts*
> *Bourbon Fudge Frosting (recipe follows)*

1. Grease well two 9-inch layer cake pans. Line the bottoms with wax paper, and grease the paper. Dust with flour, and tap out the excess. Preheat the oven to 350 degrees.

2. In the large bowl of an electric mixer cream the butter. Gradually add the sugar, and continue beating until fluffy. Blend in the cooled melted chocolate. Beat in the eggs, one at a time, beating well after each addition. Then beat in the vanilla and bourbon.

3. Sift together the flour, baking powder, and salt. On low speed add the dry ingredients to the creamed mixture alternately with the milk in three additions, beginning and ending with the flour mixture. Beat after each only until smooth. Fold in the nuts.

4. Turn the batter into the prepared pans, and smooth the tops. Bake for about 35 minutes, or until a pick inserted in the

center of the layers comes out clean. Cool the layers on racks for 10 minutes; then turn out and return to the racks. Carefully remove the wax paper, and allow to cool completely.

5. Prepare the fudge frosting, and spread thinly between the layers, then on the top and sides.

MAKES 12 SERVINGS.

BOURBON FUDGE FROSTING

1/2 cup (1 stick) unsalted butter
2 ounces unsweetened chocolate
1 egg, at room temperature
About 3 cups confectioners' sugar, sifted
1 teaspoon vanilla extract
1 teaspoon lemon juice
3 tablespoons bourbon
1 cup chopped pecans or black walnuts

1. Combine the butter and chocolate in a small saucepan. Place over low heat until melted. Stir to blend. Remove from the heat, and cool slightly.

2. In a mixing bowl slightly beat the egg. Beat in 1 cup of the sugar; then gradually pour the chocolate mixture into the egg mixture, beating constantly. Stir in the vanilla, lemon juice, and bourbon.

3. Gradually stir in about 2 cups of the remaining sugar, and continue beating, adding sugar as necessary, until the frosting is smooth and has a spreading consistency. Stir in the nuts.

BROWN SUGAR CHOCOLATE CAKE

This is a one-bowl cake, the batter quickly beaten by hand or in an electric mixer in two stages. The frosting is simple and easily made. Both cake and frosting are made with unsweetened chocolate.

2 cups sifted all-purpose flour
1 teaspoon baking soda
3/4 teaspoon salt
2 cups packed light brown sugar
1/2 cup vegetable shortening
1 cup buttermilk
1 teaspoon vanilla extract
3 medium-size eggs, at room temperature
2 ounces unsweetened chocolate, melted and cooled
Chocolate Frosting (recipe follows)

1. Generously grease and flour two 9-inch layer cake pans. Tap out the excess flour. Preheat the oven to 350 degrees.

2. Sift together the flour, baking soda, and salt into a large mixing bowl. Add the sugar, pressing it through a wire sieve. Add the shortening, buttermilk, and vanilla. Beat on medium speed of an electric mixer for 2 minutes (about 150 strokes if by hand).

3. Add the eggs and the slightly cooled melted chocolate. Continue beating for 2 minutes longer (150 strokes by hand).

4. Turn the batter into the prepared pans; spread it evenly. Bake for 30 minutes, or until the tops spring back when lightly pressed. Cool the layers in the pans on racks for 15 minutes before turning out.

5. Prepare the chocolate frosting. Then place one cake layer on a cake plate. Spread a thin layer of the frosting to the edges. Place the second layer on top; then frost the top and sides with the remaining frosting, spreading it smoothly. Allow the cake to stand at room temperature until the frosting is set.

MAKES 12 SERVINGS.

CHOCOLATE FROSTING

3 ounces unsweetened chocolate, chopped into coarse pieces
3 tablespoons unsalted butter
3 cups sifted confectioners' sugar
1/8 teaspoon salt
7 tablespoons milk
1 teaspoon vanilla extract

1. Melt the chocolate with the butter in a small, heavy saucepan set over very low heat, stirring as the chocolate begins to melt. Set aside to cool slightly.

2. Combine the sugar, salt, milk, and vanilla in the bowl of an electric mixer; beat until smooth. Add the melted chocolate mixture, and continue beating until thick enough to spread. Use immediately.

PEANUT BUTTER CHOCOLATE CAKE

A one-bowl cake, and an economical one, made without eggs and a minimum of butter.

> 1 3/4 cups sifted cake flour
> 3/4 teaspoon baking soda
> 3/4 teaspoon salt
> 1 cup sugar
> 2 tablespoons softened butter
> 3 tablespoons creamy-style peanut butter
> 2 ounces unsweetened chocolate, melted
> 1 cup milk
> 1 teaspoon vanilla extract
> Toasted Peanut Frosting (recipe follows)
> Chopped toasted peanuts, for optional garnish

1. Grease two 8-inch layer cake pans. Line with rounds of wax paper; then grease the paper. Preheat the oven to 350 degrees.

2. Sift together the flour, baking soda, salt, and sugar three times; set aside.

3. In a large mixing bowl cream the butter and peanut butter until well blended. (Use a wooden spoon for this and for blending in the remaining ingredients.)

4. Add the warm melted chocolate, and mix well. Add the sifted flour mixture, milk, and vanilla. Stir until all the flour is dampened. Then beat vigorously for 1 minute, or until thick and smooth, scraping down the sides and bottom of the bowl two or three times.

5. Turn the batter into the prepared pans, dividing it evenly. Spread to the edges of the pan to level. Bake for 23 to 25 minutes, or until the edges begin to pull away and a pick comes out clean. Cool in the pans on racks for 10 minutes; then turn out and cool completely.

6. Prepare the frosting. Spread between the layers and on the top and sides; garnish with the extra peanuts, if desired. (The tops of the layers will be slightly rounded; assemble so that the bottoms are together when being filled.)

Note: There will be barely enough frosting to glaze the cake, so be sparing with the amount between the layers.

7. Allow the cake to stand covered for at least 24 hours before serving. If it is served without being mellowed, there will be a slight taste of the baking soda.

MAKES 8 OR MORE SERVINGS.

TOASTED PEANUT FROSTING

2 tablespoons vegetable shortening
1 tablespoon unsalted butter
1 ounce unsweetened chocolate
2 cups confectioners' sugar, sifted
1/3 cup hot milk
1/2 teaspoon vanilla extract
1/2 cup toasted salted peanuts, chopped

1. Melt together the shortening, butter, and chocolate in a saucepan set over low heat; stir to blend.

2. Combine the sugar and salt in a mixing bowl. Add the hot milk, stirring until the sugar is dissolved. Blend in the vanilla and the chocolate mixture. Beat with a wooden spoon until the mixture is smooth and begins to thicken. Add the chopped peanuts, and continue beating until thick enough to spread. Use immediately.

MISSISSIPPI MUD CAKE

A cake so rich that it almost tastes like candy. Think of a cocoa cake containing pecans and coconut, topped with melted toasted marshmallows and a smooth chocolate icing, and you have the idea. It is an ideal cake to make in advance because it tastes best when stored overnight before serving.

> 1 cup (2 sticks) unsalted butter, softened
> 2 cups sugar
> 4 eggs, at room temperature
> 1 1/2 cups sifted all-purpose flour
> 1/2 teaspoon salt
> 1/3 cup unsweetened cocoa powder
> 1/2 cup coarse-chopped pecans
> 1 cup flaked coconut
> 1 teaspoon vanilla extract
> 3 cups miniature marshmallows
> Mississippi Mud Cake Frosting (recipe follows)

1. Grease and flour a 13 × 9 × 2-inch baking pan. Preheat the oven to 350 degrees.

2. In a large mixing bowl cream the butter and sugar until light. Add the eggs, one at a time, beating well after each addition. Sift together the flour, salt, and cocoa; stir into the creamed mixture. Add the pecans, coconut, and vanilla; beat well.

3. Turn the batter into the prepared pan, and smooth the top. Bake for 30 to 35 minutes. Test with a wooden pick. Remove from the oven, and sprinkle the top evenly with the marshmallows. Return to the oven, and bake briefly until the marshmallows are melted and slightly toasted. Remove the pan from the oven, and place on a rack to cool for 20 minutes.

4. Prepare the frosting, and spread over the top of the warm cake. Let stand until cold, or for best flavor allow to stand

for at least 12 hours, covering the pan when the cake is cold. Cut into about 2 1/2-inch squares for serving.

MAKES 15 SERVINGS.

MISSISSIPPI MUD CAKE FROSTING

1/2 cup (1 stick) unsalted butter
1 pound confectioners' sugar
1/3 cup unsweetened cocoa powder
1/3 cup evaporated milk

Melt the butter in a large saucepan. Sift together the sugar and cocoa into a large mixing bowl. Stir half the mixture into the melted butter along with the milk. Pour this hot mixture over the remaining sugar mixture, and beat well. Use immediately.

SOUTHERN CHOCOLATE SHEET CAKE

A popular southern specialty, the recipe for this cake appears in varying versions in many regional cookbooks. And no wonder, since it is easily made and delicious. While the cake bakes, the pecan frosting is prepared, then spread over the top just as the cake comes from the oven. The cake stays moist and fresh for a week.

> *2 cups sugar*
> *2 cups sifted all-purpose flour*
> *1/4 teaspoon salt*
> *1/2 cup unsalted margarine or vegetable shortening*
> *1 cup water*
> *1/3 cup unsweetened cocoa powder*
> *1 teaspoon baking soda*
> *1/2 cup buttermilk*
> *1 teaspoon vanilla extract*
> *2 eggs, at room temperature*
> *Cocoa Pecan Frosting (recipe follows)*

1. Grease a roasting pan, approximately $15 \times 11 \times 2$ inches. Preheat the oven to 375 degrees, setting a rack in the center.

2. Sift together the sugar, flour, and salt into a large mixing bowl. (This cake may be beaten by hand with a wooden spoon or prepared in an electric mixer at low speed.)

3. Melt the margarine with the water and cocoa in a small saucepan over medium-high heat, stirring and bringing just to a boil. Pour over the dry ingredients, and mix well.

4. Stir the baking soda into the buttermilk along with the vanilla until dissolved. Add to the cocoa mixture, stirring well.

5. Add the eggs, beating them slightly before adding if using a wooden spoon. Or add without beating if using electric beaters, and beat them just until thoroughly combined.

6. Pour the mixture into the prepared pan, smoothing the

batter evenly. Bake for about 20 to 25 minutes, or until the center springs back with the slightest touch or a wooden pick comes out clean.

7. While the cake is baking, prepare the frosting. When the cake comes from the oven, let it stand for 10 minutes; then spread the frosting over the top evenly to the edges. Let the cake cool completely in the pan. Cut into about 2 1/2-inch squares for serving.

MAKES 24 SERVINGS.

COCOA PECAN FROSTING

1/2 cup (1 stick) margarine
1/4 cup unsweetened cocoa powder
1/3 cup buttermilk
4 cups (1 pound) confectioners' sugar
1 teaspoon vanilla extract
1/4 teaspoon salt
1 cup chopped pecans

Combine the margarine, cocoa, and buttermilk in a large, heavy saucepan. Bring just to a boil, stirring to blend evenly. Remove from the heat, and add the sugar, vanilla, and salt; beat until smooth; then stir in the pecans. Let stand until ready to frost the cake.

SELF-ICED COCOA CAKE

What cake could be simpler to make? One bowl and a wooden spoon for mixing, one pan for baking, and the icing baked along with the batter.

> 1 1/4 cups sifted cake flour
> 3 tablespoons unsweetened cocoa powder
> 1 1/2 teaspoons baking powder
> 1/4 teaspoon salt
> 1/4 cup (1/2 stick) unsalted butter, softened
> 1 cup sugar
> 2 eggs, at room temperature
> 1/2 cup milk
> 1 teaspoon vanilla extract
> 4 ounces dark sweet chocolate, grated (page 9)
> 1/2 cup coarse-chopped walnuts
> Vanilla or other flavor ice cream (optional)

1. Grease and flour an 8-inch-square baking pan. Heat the oven to 350 degrees.

2. Sift together the flour, cocoa, baking powder, and salt. Set aside.

3. Combine the butter and sugar in a large mixing bowl. Beat with a wooden spoon until creamy. Add the eggs, one at a time, and beat until the mixture is light and smooth.

4. Add the flour mixture with the milk, alternating a little of each so that the mixture blends after each addition. Add the vanilla, and beat until light.

5. Pour the batter into the prepared pan. Sprinkle the grated chocolate evenly over the top; then sprinkle the walnuts over the chocolate; press in lightly.

6. Bake for 35 to 40 minutes, or until the cake pulls slightly away from the edges of the pan. The batter will puff and rise unevenly; that is characteristic of this type of cake.

Cool the cake on a rack just until it has cooled for easy cutting. It should be cut into squares and served warm with the chocolate meltingly soft. Serve plain or with a scoop of vanilla ice cream or other flavor of your choice.

Note: For leftovers, reheat the cake in the pan, covered with foil, until the chocolate softens.

MAKES 9 OR MORE SERVINGS.

DOUBLE CHOCOLATE CUPCAKES

Velvety cake and generous, rich, and glossy frosting are combined here to make the perfect chocolate cupcake.

> 1/4 cup vegetable shortening
> 1 cup sugar
> 2 eggs, at room temperature
> 2 ounces unsweetened chocolate, melted and cooled
> 1 teaspoon vanilla extract
> 1 cup sifted all-purpose flour
> 1 teaspoon baking powder
> 1/8 teaspoon salt
> 1/2 cup milk
> **Rich and Glossy Chocolate Frosting (recipe follows)**

1. Line 2 1/2-inch cupcake pans with paper liners (the batter will fill 18). Preheat the oven to 375 degrees, setting one rack just above and one rack just below the center.

2. Using a large mixing bowl and a wooden spoon, blend the shortening and the sugar until creamy. Add the eggs, one at a time, and beat until light. Blend in the melted chocolate and vanilla.

3. Sift the flour with the baking powder and salt. Add alternately with the milk to the chocolate mixture, stirring only long enough to mix after each addition.

4. Spoon the batter into the cupcake liners, so that each is evenly filled. Then bake for about 15 to 18 minutes, or until the cupcakes test done with a wooden pick. Let cool for about 5 minutes; then remove from the pans, and cool completely before frosting.

5. Prepare the frosting. Then spread it over the cupcakes, swirling the tops attractively.

Note: Protected with the liners and the covering of frosting, leftovers keep well at room temperature for a day or two.

MAKES 18 CUPCAKES.

RICH AND GLOSSY CHOCOLATE FROSTING

1 tablespoon unsalted butter
2 tablespoons vegetable shortening
3 ounces unsweetened chocolate, chopped into coarse pieces
1 1/2 cups confectioners' sugar, sifted
Scant 1/4 teaspoon salt
1/4 cup hot milk
1/2 teaspoon vanilla extract

1. Melt the butter and shortening with the chocolate in a heavy saucepan set over low heat. Stir to blend; set aside.

2. Combine the sugar and salt in a mixing bowl. Add the hot milk, stirring with a wooden spoon until the sugar is dissolved. Blend in first the vanilla, then the chocolate mixture. Beat with a wooden spoon only until smooth and thick enough to spread. Use immediately to frost the cupcakes.

CHOCOLATE TOWN SYRUP CUPCAKES

Store-bought chocolate syrup makes these cupcakes easy to make. They are topped with a contrasting white and fluffy frosting.

> 1/2 cup unsalted butter, softened
> 1 cup sugar
> 1 teaspoon vanilla extract
> 4 eggs, at room temperature
> 1 1/2 cups unsifted all-purpose flour
> 1/2 teaspoon baking soda
> 1/4 teaspoon salt
> 1 1/2 cups (16-ounce can) chocolate syrup,* at room
>   temperature
> Fluffy White Frosting (recipe follows)

1. Line 2 1/2-inch cupcake pans with paper liners (the batter will fill 30). Preheat the oven to 375 degrees.

2. Cream the butter, sugar, and vanilla until light and fluffy. Add the eggs, one at a time, beating well after each addition. Sift together the flour, baking soda, and salt; add alternately with the chocolate syrup to the creamed mixture, beating only long enough to blend after each addition.

3. Fill the cupcake liners with the batter, each half-full. Bake for 18 to 20 minutes, or until a wooden pick comes out clean. Let cool for about 5 minutes; then remove from the pans, and cool completely.

4. Prepare the frosting, and spread it generously over the cupcake tops, swirling it attractively.

MAKES 2 1/2 DOZEN CUPCAKES.

*Hershey's chocolate syrup was used in the testing of this recipe.

FLUFFY WHITE FROSTING

1/3 cup water
1 tablespoon light corn syrup
1 cup sugar
1/4 teaspoon cream of tartar
1/4 teaspoon salt
1 egg white, at room temperature
1 teaspoon vanilla extract

1. Combine the water, corn syrup, sugar, cream of tartar, and salt in a heavy saucepan. Place over moderate heat. Stir until the sugar dissolves and bubbles appear around the edge of the saucepan. Remove from the heat.

2. Whip the egg white, using electric beaters set at medium speed, until stiff but not dry. Pour the hot syrup into the egg white in a fine stream, beating constantly. Add the vanilla, and continue beating for about 5 minutes, or until the frosting loses its shiny appearance and stands in stiff peaks. Use immediately.

CHOCOLATE CREAM CHEESE CUPCAKES

Moist dark chocolate cupcakes with a pale chocolate frosting made with cream cheese.

> *1 1/2 cups sifted all-purpose flour*
> *1 cup sugar*
> *3 tablespoons unsweetened cocoa powder*
> *1 teaspoon baking soda*
> *1/2 teaspoon salt*
> *1 cup cold water*
> *1/4 cup plus 2 tablespoons vegetable oil*
> *1 tablespoon white vinegar*
> *1 teaspoon vanilla extract*
> **Cream Cheese Frosting (recipe follows)**

1. Preheat the oven to 375 degrees. Line 2 1/2-inch muffin tins with cupcake papers (the batter will fill 15).

2. Sift the flour, sugar, cocoa, baking soda, and salt into a medium-size mixing bowl. Make a well in the center. Add the water, oil, vinegar, and vanilla. Stir with a fork until smooth. Do not beat. (The batter will be thin.)

3. Fill the cupcake papers about two-thirds full with the batter. Bake for about 18 to 20 minutes, or until a pick inserted in the center comes out clean. Cool in the pans on racks. Then frost the tops with the frosting. Cover and refrigerate before serving.

MAKES 15 CUPCAKES.

CREAM CHEESE FROSTING

3 ounces cream cheese, at room temperature
6 tablespoons (3/4 stick) unsalted butter, softened
2 teaspoons milk
1/2 teaspoon vanilla extract
1 ounce unsweetened chocolate, melted
2 cups confectioners' sugar, sifted

Place the cream cheese in a mixing bowl; beat until creamy; then blend in the butter. Add the milk, vanilla, and chocolate. Gradually stir in the sugar; then beat until creamy.

IV

SPECIALTY CAKES AND TORTES

VIENNA SPECKLE TORTE

ITALIAN SPONGE TORTE

GRASSHOPPER CREAM LAYER CAKE

BLACK FOREST KIRSCH TORTE

EIGHT-LAYER DOUBLE CHOCOLATE TORTE

FRENCH CHOCOLATE GENOISE

AUSTRIAN SIX-LAYER APRICOT TORTE

BROWNIE RIBBON CAKE

CHOCOLATE PECAN UPSIDE-DOWN CAKE

CONTINENTAL CHOCOLATE CAKE

HUNGARIAN CHOCOLATE WALNUT TORTE

CHOCOLATE SIN

LE GÂTEAU VICTOIRE

CHOCOLATE CREAM CAKE DELUXE

GALETTE AU CHOCOLAT

CURRANT CHOCOLATE WHISKY CAKE

BELGIAN CHOCOLATE CAKE

VIENNESE CHOCOLATE ALMOND TORTE

BAVARIAN CHOCOLATE PECAN TORTE

CHOCOLATE ALMOND MOUSSE TORTE

VIENNA SPECKLE TORTE

An airy sponge cake made with grated chocolate—the speckles—with fresh strawberries in the filling and as garnish. A pretty presentation, especially if the strawberries are first dipped in chocolate.

> *3/4 cup sifted cake flour*
> *4 ounces unsweetened chocolate, grated (page 9)*
> *6 large eggs, separated, plus 1 egg white, at room temperature*
> *1 cup sugar*
> *3/4 teaspoon vanilla extract*
> *1/4 teaspoon almond extract*
> *1/4 teaspoon salt*
> *1/4 teaspoon cream of tartar*
> *Fresh Strawberry Cream Filling and Frosting (recipe follows)*

1. Preheat the oven to 350 degrees, placing a rack in the lower third of the oven. Have ready an ungreased 9- or 10-inch tube pan.

2. Sift the flour again into a small mixing bowl. Add the grated chocolate, blend, and set aside.

3. In a large bowl, with electric beaters, beat the egg yolks until fluffy. Gradually add the sugar, and continue beating until the mixture is thick enough to form a ribbon when the beaters are lifted. Add the vanilla and almond extracts and half the flour mixture. Beat on low speed, briefly but until thoroughly mixed.

4. In a separate bowl beat the egg whites with the salt and cream of tartar until stiff but not dry. Sprinkle the remaining flour mixture over the top, and fold in with a rubber spatula, only until lightly mixed. Then stir a little into the egg yolk mixture to lighten it; and fold in the remainder gently but thoroughly.

5. Turn the batter into the pan; shake slightly to level; then bake for 45 minutes, or until a pick comes out clean. In-

vert the cake in the pan on a rack to cool for an hour. Loosen the cake by running a thin knife between the cake and the sides of the pan in one long, steady stroke. Remove the bottom of the pan and release the tube in the same manner. Invert the cake onto a serving platter, and let it stand until completely cooled.

6. Using a serrated knife, cut the cake horizontally into two layers. Spread about one-third of the whipped cream (see recipe below) over the bottom layer, and press in the cut berries. Spread the surrounding cream to cover them completely. (If necessary, add a little more whipped cream.) Place the second layer, cut side down, firmly on top. Then spread the entire cake with the remaining cream.

7. For garnish, set the reserved whole berries in a circle around the top edge of the frosted cake. Refrigerate until serving, several hours if desired.

Note: Chocolate Dipped Strawberries (page 14) make an especially attractive garnish. Have them at room temperature; then garnish the torte just before serving.

MAKES 10 TO 12 SERVINGS.

FRESH STRAWBERRY CREAM FILLING AND FROSTING

> *1 pint small, fresh strawberries*
> *2 cups heavy cream*
> *1 teaspoon vanilla extract*
> *1/4 cup confectioners' sugar*

1. Rinse the strawberries, and let them dry on paper toweling. Set aside 10 to 12 berries for garnish. Remove the stems from the remainder; then cut into halves, or quarters if large; set aside.

2. In a large chilled bowl and with chilled beaters, whip the cream with the vanilla and sugar until the cream is firm enough to hold a definite shape. Use immediately.

ITALIAN SPONGE TORTE

Four thin golden sponge cake layers moistened with sweet Italian vermouth, filled and topped with chocolate whipped cream and a garnish of toasted almonds. A special dessert that may be made in stages: the cake a day or two in advance, then the completed torte refrigerated for several hours.

> 1 cup sifted cake flour
> 3/4 teaspoon baking powder
> 1/4 teaspoon salt
> 1/2 cup cold water
> 2 large eggs, separated, at room temperature
> 1 cup sugar
> 1 teaspoon vanilla extract
> 1/2 teaspoon lemon extract
> Chocolate Whipped Cream Frosting (recipe follows)
> 3 tablespoons sweet Italian vermouth
> 1/4 cup slivered blanched almonds, toasted (page 20)

1. Grease only the bottoms of two 8-inch-round layer cake pans. Line the bottoms with wax paper, and grease the paper. Preheat the oven to 350 degrees, setting a rack in the center.

2. Sift together the flour, baking powder, and salt three times; set aside.

3. Combine the water and egg yolks in a large mixer bowl. Beat at medium speed to a thick foam; then gradually beat in the sugar, and continue beating at the same speed for about 10 minutes, or until the mixture is pale, thick, and creamy. Remove the bowl from the mixer, and sprinkle the flour mixture over the top; fold in with a rubber spatula. Then fold in the vanilla and lemon extracts.

4. Beat the egg whites until they form moist, stiff peaks. Quickly fold them into the egg yolk batter. Pour the batter into the prepared pans, dividing it evenly. Tap the pans lightly on the counter once or twice to eliminate any large air bubbles.

5. Bake for 25 minutes, or until the tops of the cakes are golden brown and spring back lightly to the touch. Invert the pans on cake racks, and let them stand until cold. Run a knife around the edges; then turn out the layers. (If they seem to stick, rap hard on the pan once to release.) Carefully peel off the wax paper. Place in plastic bags to prevent drying. (They will keep well for a day or two.)

6. To assemble, first prepare the frosting; then refrigerate. Using a serrated knife, cut each cake layer horizontally into halves, making four in all.

7. Place one layer, crust side down, on a cake plate. Sprinkle 1 tablespoon of the vermouth over the top; then spread part (about 1/2 cup) of the whipped cream over the top. Place a second layer, cut side up, on top, and repeat the procedure, ending with crust side up on the last layer. Spread the remaining frosting over the top (the sides are not frosted). Sprinkle the almonds over the top. Refrigerate for at least 4 hours before serving, but no longer than 10 hours. Serve chilled, cut into wedges.

MAKES 8 OR MORE SERVINGS.

CHOCOLATE WHIPPED CREAM FROSTING

1 cup heavy cream
1/2 cup chocolate syrup,* chilled

In a chilled bowl, with chilled beaters, whip the cream until it begins to thicken. Gradually beat in the chocolate syrup, and continue beating until the mixture mounds softly but holds a shape thick enough to spread. Refrigerate briefly until ready to use.

*Hershey's chocolate syrup was used in the testing of this recipe.

GRASSHOPPER CREAM LAYER CAKE

A four-layer cake, filled and frosted with whipped cream tinted green and "spiked" with crème de menthe and crème de cacao liqueurs—just like the popular after-dinner drinks. The chocolate-flavored layers are nearly white in color because the batter is made with white chocolate.

> **1/2 cup (1 stick) unsalted butter, softened**
> **1 cup sugar**
> **1/2 teaspoon vanilla extract**
> **2 cups sifted cake flour**
> **3 teaspoons baking powder**
> **1 teaspoon salt**
> **1 cup milk**
> **3 ounces white chocolate, grated (page 9)***
> **3 egg whites**
> **Grasshopper Filling and Frosting (recipe follows)**
> **Chocolate scrolls (page 11), for optional garnish**

1. Preheat the oven to 350 degrees. Grease and flour two 8 × 1 1/2-inch-round layer cake pans.

2. In a large mixing bowl, with electric beaters, cream together thoroughly the butter and 1/2 cup of the sugar. Beat in the vanilla.

3. Sift together the flour, baking powder, and salt. Add alternately with the milk to the creamed mixture, beginning and ending with the dry ingredients and beating well after each addition. Stir in the grated white chocolate.

4. Beat the egg whites until soft peaks form; then add the remaining 1/2 cup sugar, a tablespoon at a time, and beat just until the mixture holds a firm, soft peak. In two or three additions, gently fold into the batter, just long enough to incorporate.

*White chocolate is sold in bulk at confectionary stores or as imported small bars in gourmet shops.

5. Turn the batter into the prepared pans, dividing it evenly and spreading it to the sides; shake the pans slightly to level the batter. Bake for 25 to 30 minutes, or until the centers spring back when lightly touched and the cakes begin to pull slightly away from the edges of the pans. Remove from the oven to wire racks to cool for at least 5 minutes; then turn out onto racks to cool thoroughly.

6. When the layers are cooled, split each in half horizontally with a serrated knife to make four layers. Prepare the filling and frosting.

7. Place one of the layers, cut side up, on a cake plate, and spread with some of the frosting, about 1/3 to 1/2 inch thick. Place a second layer, cut side down, on top; spread with more frosting. Repeat with the remaining layers. Cover the top and sides with the remaining frosting, swirling it decoratively. (If desired, decorate the top of the cake with chocolate scrolls.) Refrigerate until ready to serve.

Note: The cake may be made a day or two in advance as the frosting holds up well.

MAKES 10 TO 12 SERVINGS.

GRASSHOPPER FILLING AND FROSTING

1 envelope unflavored gelatin
1/4 cup cold water
1/3 cup green crème de menthe, a mint-flavored liqueur
1/3 cup white crème de cacao, a chocolate-flavored liqueur
2 cups heavy cream

1. Sprinkle the gelatin over the cold water in a small saucepan. Let stand a few minutes to soften; then stir in the liqueurs. Stir over low heat just until the gelatin is dissolved; set aside to cool to room temperature but not long enough to set. (To cool it rapidly, place the saucepan in a pan of cold water with ice cubes; stir until cooled.)

2. In a large mixer bowl whip the cream until it thickens slightly. Gradually pour in the gelatin mixture in a steady stream, while beating; continue to beat until the cream is thick enough to spread as frosting. (Do not overbeat, or the cream will turn buttery.) Use immediately.

BLACK FOREST KIRSCH TORTE

An elegant four-layer brandy-flavored dessert. The cake layers are choc-
olate and are alternately topped with ribbons of chocolate almond filling
and whipped cream.

2 1/4 cups plus 2 tablespoons sifted all-purpose flour
2 1/4 cups plus 2 tablespoons sugar
1 1/4 teaspoons baking soda
1 teaspoon salt
1/4 teaspoon baking powder
2/3 cup (1 1/3 sticks) unsalted butter, softened
4 ounces unsweetened chocolate, melted and cooled
1 cup plus 2 tablespoons water
2 tablespoons kirsch or light rum
3 eggs
Chocolate Almond Filling (recipe follows)
Whipped Cream Filling (recipe follows)
Chocolate scrolls (page 11), for garnish
12 red candied cherries, for garnish

1. Grease generously, then flour the bottoms and sides of
two 9-inch layer cake pans. Preheat the oven to 350 degrees.

2. Sift together into a large mixer bowl the flour, sugar,
baking soda, salt, and baking powder. Add the butter, melted
chocolate, water, and kirsch. Beat at low speed just long
enough to blend; continue beating at medium speed for 2 minutes, scraping the sides and the bottom of the bowl after 1 minute. Add the eggs, and beat for 2 minutes longer.

3. Turn the batter into the prepared cake pans, dividing
and spreading it evenly. Bake for about 35 minutes, or until a
wooden pick comes out clean. Cool on racks for 10 minutes.
Then run a knife around the sides to release the layers, and turn
out. Cool completely.

4. When the layers are cold, split them horizontally to
make four layers in all. Prepare the fillings.

5. To assemble the torte, place one cake layer, cut side up, on a serving plate. Spread with half the chocolate filling. Set the next layer, cut side down, on top, and spread with half the cream filling. Repeat the layers, ending with the cream. Then garnish the top center with chocolate scrolls. (Note that the sides of the torte are left plain.) Arrange the cherries around the top edge.

6. Before serving, refrigerate the torte for several hours, preferably overnight.

MAKES 12 SERVINGS.

CHOCOLATE ALMOND FILLING

6 ounces dark sweet chocolate, chopped into coarse pieces
3/4 cup (1 1/2 sticks) unsalted butter, softened
1/2 cup chopped toasted almonds (page 20)

Melt the chocolate in a saucepan set over very low heat. Cool slightly; then beat in the butter, a chunk at a time. When the mixture is blended, stir in the nuts. (If necessary, reheat briefly to bring to a spreading consistency before using.)

WHIPPED CREAM FILLING

1 1/2 cups heavy cream
6 tablespoons confectioners' sugar
3 tablespoons kirsch or light rum

In a chilled bowl with chilled beaters, whip the cream with the sugar until soft peaks form. Then add the kirsch, and continue beating until stiff but not buttery.

EIGHT-LAYER DOUBLE CHOCOLATE TORTE

A European-style torte with nearly as much frosting as there is cake. The layers are thin, the frosting is thick, and when the two are combined and chilled, they seem to meld together.

3/4 cup sifted cake flour
1/2 teaspoon baking powder
1/2 teaspoon salt
4 large eggs, at room temperature
3/4 cup plus 2 tablespoons sugar
2 1/2 ounces unsweetened chocolate, chopped into coarse
  pieces
1/4 cup cold water
1/4 teaspoon baking soda
Confectioners' sugar
Creamy Chocolate Frosting (recipe follows)

1. Line the bottom of a greased 15 1/2 × 10 1/2 × 1-inch jelly roll pan with a sheet of wax paper; grease the top. Preheat the oven to 350 degrees, setting a rack in the center.

2. Sift together the flour, baking powder, and salt; set aside.

3. Place the eggs in the large bowl of an electric mixer. At medium-high speed beat in the 3/4 cup sugar, one tablespoon at a time. Continue beating for about 10 minutes, or until the mixture has thickened and tripled in volume. Remove the bowl from the mixer, and add the sifted flour mixture (all at once). Fold in with a wire whisk or rubber spatula, folding carefully to prevent deflating.

4. Melt the chocolate in a heavy saucepan set over very low heat. Remove from the heat, and immediately stir in the cold water, baking soda, and remaining 2 tablespoons sugar. Stir until thick and smooth. Then add to the batter, and quickly blend in.

5. Turn the batter into the prepared pan, spreading it evenly. Bake for 18 to 20 minutes, or until the top springs back when lightly touched.

6. While the cake is baking, place a cloth towel on a flat surface, and sprinkle with confectioners' sugar. When the cake is done, immediately invert the pan onto the sugared towel. Remove the pan, and carefully peel off the wax paper. Trim the crisp edges with a sharp knife. Cool.

7. Cut the cake once across and once lengthwise to make four equal parts. Split each quarter horizontally through the middle, making eight thin layers.

8. Put the layers together with the frosting, using about 1/4 cup frosting between each layer. Cover the top and the sides of the torte with the remaining frosting, swirling it decoratively.

Note: As the layers are put together with the frosting, they may tend to move out of alignment; to hold them in place, use toothpicks as necessary.

9. Before serving, refrigerate the torte for several hours, overnight if preferred. Cut across into thin slices for serving.

MAKES 12 GENEROUS SERVINGS.

CREAMY CHOCOLATE FROSTING

4 1/2 ounces unsweetened chocolate, chopped into coarse
 pieces
1/2 cup (1 stick) unsalted butter
3 cups sifted confectioners' sugar
1/3 cup milk
2 egg whites, at room temperature
1 teaspoon vanilla extract

1. Place the chocolate and butter in the top of a double boiler; set over simmering water, and stir until the ingredients

are melted and blended. Remove from the heat, and add the sugar, milk, egg whites, and vanilla in that order; mix well.

2. Set the pan in a bowl of ice water, and beat with hand-held beaters at medium speed until the mixture is creamy and thick enough to spread.

Note: This frosting is easy to work with because it is soft and moist. It will remain creamy once the torte has been frosted and refrigerated.

FRENCH CHOCOLATE GENOISE

This buttery French chocolate sponge cake can be made in one bowl and is leavened entirely with air incorporated by beating. The layers are filled and frosted generously with a wonderfully rich and extravagant chocolate buttercream. A French classic.

> 6 large eggs, at room temperature
> 1 cup sugar
> 1/2 cup sifted cake flour
> 1/2 cup unsweetened cocoa powder
> 6 tablespoons crème de cacao or other chocolate liqueur
> 1/2 cup (1 stick) unsalted butter, melted and cooled
> Chocolate Buttercream (recipe follows)
> 3 tablespoons chocolate sprinkles (page 13), for garnish

1. Grease well two 9-inch-round layer cake pans; dust with flour, and tap out the excess. Preheat the oven to 350 degrees, setting a rack in the center. Have all ingredients and equipment at a warm room temperature to ensure success.

2. Beat the eggs and sugar at high speed in a large electric mixer bowl for 10 to 15 minutes, or until they triple in bulk and look like whipped cream. Remove from the mixer.

3. Sift the flour and cocoa together, several times if necessary so that they are well blended. Sprinkle about 1/4 cup at a time over the egg batter, folding in with a rubber spatula, gently but not completely after each addition. The last addition should be folded in thoroughly.

4. Stir 2 tablespoons of the crème de cacao into the butter, which should be tepid, not cold. Add a couple of heaping tablespoons of the egg mixture, and stir lightly until blended. Pour back over the batter, and fold in gently but thoroughly.

5. Pour the batter into the prepared pans. Firmly tap the pans once on a counter to remove large air bubbles. Bake for about 30 minutes, or until the cakes pull well away from the

sides of the pans and the tops are springy to the touch. Remove from the pans immediately, and cool on wire racks.

6. When the layers are cooled, brush the tops with the remaining 4 tablespoons of the crème de cacao. Split each cake horizontally to make four layers.

7. Prepare the buttercream as directed. Place one of the cake layers, bottom side down, on a serving plate. Spread with a layer of the buttercream, making it about 1/3 inch thick. Repeat with the remaining layers, ending with a liqueur-saturated layer on top. Spread this layer and the sides of the torte with the remaining buttercream, spreading it smoothly or swirling it into peaks. Garnish the top with the chocolate sprinkles.

Note: For a more attractive presentation, spread a thin layer of the buttercream over the top of the cake; with a pastry bag fitted with a large star tube, make a ring of rosettes to cover the top of the cake. Then use the remainder to frost the sides, and garnish as directed.

8. Refrigerate the torte for at least a few hours or overnight. Remove from the refrigerator about an hour or so before serving, long enough so that the buttercream returns to its creamy state, firm but somewhat softened.

MAKES 12 SERVINGS.

CHOCOLATE BUTTERCREAM

6 ounces semisweet chocolate, chopped into coarse pieces
1/4 cup plus 1/3 cup water
4 egg yolks, at room temperature
1 cup sugar
1/4 teaspoon cream of tartar
1 1/2 cups (3 sticks) unsalted butter, softened
2 tablespoons crème de cacao, or other chocolate liqueur

1. Melt the chocolate with the 1/4 cup water in a small saucepan set over very low heat. Stir until smooth, and set aside.

2. In a mixer bowl, with electric beaters, beat the egg yolks until foamy. Set aside.

3. Combine the sugar, 1/3 cup water, and cream of tartar in a small, heavy saucepan; set over medium heat, and stir until the sugar dissolves and the liquid comes to a boil. Let the syrup boil, without stirring, until it reaches 217 to 220 degrees on a candy thermometer. (This will occur within minutes.) Remove the pan from the heat.

4. Gradually beat the hot syrup into the egg yolks with the mixer set at medium speed; then beat at high speed for about 5 to 6 minutes, or until the mixture is cool and has the consistency of light mayonnaise, the batter barely forming a ribbon that quickly dissolves.

5. Reduce the speed to medium, and blend in the chocolate. Add the butter, 1 to 2 tablespoons at a time, and continue beating until the last addition is well blended. Beat in the crème de cacao. The buttercream will be smooth, light, and creamy and will keep well at room temperature until ready to use.

AUSTRIAN SIX-LAYER APRICOT TORTE

A beautiful specialty torte filled and frosted with chocolate buttercream and apricot glaze, layer upon layer so that it is almost four inches high. The cake layers are buttery, golden, and moist with apricot preserves.

1/2 cup plus 2/3 cup apricot preserves*
1 tablespoon lemon juice
1 cup (2 sticks) unsalted butter, softened
1 1/2 teaspoons vanilla extract
1 1/2 cups sugar
3 extra-large eggs, at room temperature
3 cups sifted cake flour
2 teaspoons baking powder
1/2 teaspoon baking soda
1 teaspoon salt
3/4 cup plus 2 tablespoons milk
Bittersweet Chocolate Buttercream (recipe follows)

1. Grease only the bottoms of three 8-inch layer cake pans with unsalted butter or shortening. Line the bottoms with wax paper and grease the paper; dust with flour, tapping out the excess. Adjust two racks, one just above and one just below the center of the oven, to accommodate the three pans. Preheat the oven to 350 degrees.

2. Combine the 1/2 cup apricot preserves and lemon juice. (Chop any large pieces; the mixture should be fairly smooth.) Set aside.

3. In an electric mixer bowl cream together the butter and vanilla. At medium speed gradually beat in the sugar, and con-

*The least expensive jars of preserves are best here. They tend to contain only small bits of apricot; more costly preserves with larger pieces will necessitate using an extra chopping procedure.

tinue to beat until the mixture is light and fluffy. Beat in the apricot preserve mixture.

4. Add the eggs one at a time, beating well after each addition.

5. Sift together the flour, baking powder, baking soda, and salt. With the mixer set at low speed, alternately add the flour mixture in fourths and the milk in thirds, beating after each addition only until blended.

6. Turn the batter equally into the pans, and spread it evenly. Bake for about 30 minutes, or until a wooden pick inserted in the centers comes out clean. (Do not underbake, or the layers may stick to the wax paper when they are turned out and the paper is removed.) Cool on racks for 10 minutes; then invert onto the racks; carefully peel away the paper, and allow to cool completely.

7. Using a serrated knife, split each layer horizontally to make two layers, six in all.

8. Heat the 2/3 cup apricot preserves in a small saucepan just long enough to thin. Press the mixture through a wire sieve onto the crust sides of two of the cake layers, dividing it evenly. Spread smoothly to the edges. Set aside.

9. Prepare the chocolate buttercream. Place one of the cake layers, crust side down, on a serving plate. Spread thinly with the frosting; repeat with another layer. Then place one of the glazed layers on top. Add the fourth and fifth layers, spreading each with the frosting; then set the remaining glazed layer on top. Use the remaining frosting to ice the sides.

Note: It is important that the frosting be spread in a thin coat over the layers, so that there will be enough to frost the sides.

10. Refrigerate the torte for several hours to set the frosting; but bring it close to room temperature before serving. It should be cut with a sharp, heavy knife.

MAKES 12 OR MORE SERVINGS.

BITTERSWEET CHOCOLATE BUTTERCREAM

5 ounces unsweetened chocolate, chopped into coarse pieces
4 egg yolks, at room temperature
1/2 cup sugar
1/4 cup water
2 teaspoons instant coffee powder or 1 teaspoon instant
  espresso
1/2 cup (1 stick) unsalted butter, softened

1. Melt the chocolate in a small saucepan set over very low heat. Set aside.

2. In the small bowl of an electric mixer beat the egg yolks until foamy. Set aside.

3. Combine the sugar, water, and instant coffee in a small, heavy saucepan. Set over medium heat, and stir until the sugar has dissolved. Continue cooking until the mixture comes to a full boil.

4. With the mixer set at low speed, very slowly add the sugar syrup to the egg yolks in a fine stream; then beat at high speed for about 5 minutes, or until the mixture is cool and has the consistency of light mayonnaise, the batter barely forming a ribbon that quickly dissolves.

5. Reduce the speed to medium, and blend in the chocolate. Add the butter, a tablespoon at a time, and continue beating until the last addition is well blended and the mixture is thick enough to spread. Use immediately.

BROWNIE RIBBON CAKE

A coveted old-time recipe for brownies here turned into a simple but superb four-layer torte, which is filled and frosted with whipped cream.

4 ounces unsweetened chocolate, chopped into coarse pieces
2/3 cup (1 1/3 sticks) unsalted butter
4 large eggs, at room temperature
2 cups sugar
1 1/2 cups sifted all-purpose flour
1 teaspoon baking powder
1 teaspoon salt
1 teaspoon vanilla extract
1 cup coarse-chopped walnuts
Whipped Cream Filling and Frosting (recipe follows)
Chocolate sprinkles (page 13), for optional garnish

1. Grease a 15 1/2 × 10 1/2 × 1-inch jelly roll pan. Line the bottom and sides with a sheet of foil; grease the foil. Preheat the oven to 350 degrees, setting a rack in the center.

2. Melt the chocolate with the butter in a small, heavy saucepan over low heat, stirring occasionally. When the mixture is melted and smooth, set it aside to cool.

3. In a large bowl, using a whisk or electric beaters, beat the eggs with the sugar until light and creamy. Add the chocolate mixture, and continue to beat just until well blended.

4. Sift the flour with the baking powder and salt. Stir into the egg mixture, blending well, but do not beat. Add the vanilla and walnuts; mix in.

5. Pour the mixture into the prepared pan; shake it gently from side to side to level, making certain that the corners are not slighted. Bake for 18 to 20 minutes, reversing the pan from front to back, if necessary (toward the end), to ensure even baking. The cake is done when it seems firm to a light touch and a pick comes out just barely dry. (Do not overbake, so that it will be moist, not dry.)

6. Set the pan on a wire rack to cool completely. To remove, place a large cookie sheet over the pan; invert and lift off the pan; then carefully peel away the foil.

Note: The torte should be put together soon after cooling. To hold for a few hours, the pan or the turned-out torte should be covered with foil.

7. To assemble, first prepare the whipped cream filling and frosting. Then trim the edges of the cake so that they are even. Cut the cake across the length into four sections, each about 3 3/4 inches wide and 10 inches long. Place one of the sections on a cookie sheet, and spread with a layer of the whipped cream; repeat with the remaining layers. Then frost the top and sides with the remaining whipped cream. (Count on about half the mixture for the filling, the remainder for the frosting.) Sprinkle the top of the torte with the chocolate sprinkles. Refrigerate the torte for at least 24 hours before serving.

8. Remove the torte from the refrigerator about 30 minutes before serving. Cut across into thick slices.

MAKES 12 SERVINGS.

WHIPPED CREAM FILLING AND FROSTING

2 cups heavy cream
1/4 cup confectioners' sugar

In a chilled bowl, with chilled beaters, whip the cream with the sugar until very stiff but not buttery. Refrigerate briefly while preparing the torte layers.

CHOCOLATE PECAN UPSIDE-DOWN CAKE

A specialty cake baked in a large Bundt pan. It is served warm or at room temperature, plain or with whipped cream or ice cream.

PECAN TOPPING

1/4 cup (1/2 stick) unsalted butter
1/2 cup firm-packed brown sugar
1/2 cup light corn syrup
1 1/2 cups (6 ounces) coarse-broken pecans

CHOCOLATE CAKE

2 cups sifted all-purpose flour
1 teaspoon baking soda
1/2 teaspoon salt
1 1/2 cups granulated sugar
1/2 cup (1 stick) unsalted butter, softened
3/4 cup dairy sour cream, at room temperature
1 teaspoon vanilla extract
3 large eggs, at room temperature
3 ounces unsweetened chocolate, melted and cooled
Whipped cream or ice cream, optional

1. Grease well a 12-cup Bundt pan. (Do not use a spring-form pan with center tube.) Preheat the oven to 350 degrees, setting a rack up one-third from the bottom.

2. *For the topping:* Melt the butter in a small saucepan. Stir in the brown sugar and corn syrup. Pour into the prepared pan, spreading the mixture evenly over the bottom. Scatter the pecans evenly on top. Set aside.

3. *For the cake:* Sift together the flour, baking soda, salt and sugar into the bowl of an electric mixer. Add the butter (in chunks), sour cream, and vanilla. Blend at low speed; then beat at medium speed for 2 minutes. Add the eggs and melted chocolate. Beat for 1 minute.

4. Spoon the batter over the topping in the pan. Bake for 50 to 60 minutes, or until a wooden pick comes out clean.

5. Loosen the edges with a sharp knife; then immediately turn the pan upside down on a serving plate. Let stand for a few minutes until all the sugar-pecan mixture adheres to the cake; then remove the pan.

6. Serve slightly warm or at room temperature, either plain or with whipped cream or a compatible-flavored ice cream.

MAKES 12 OR MORE SERVINGS.

CONTINENTAL CHOCOLATE CAKE

A special single-layer rum-soaked cake with a simple whipped cream topping and chocolate garnish.

1 1/4 cups sifted all-purpose flour
2 teaspoons baking powder
1/2 teaspoon salt
1 cup packed dark brown sugar
2 eggs, separated, at room temperature
1/2 cup milk
1/3 cup vegetable oil
2 ounces unsweetened chocolate, melted and cooled
1 1/2 teaspoons vanilla extract
3/4 cup dark corn syrup
1/4 cup light or dark rum
Sweetened Whipped Cream Topping (recipe follows)
Chocolate scrolls (page 11) or chocolate shavings (page 12),
   for garnish

1. Grease a 9-inch-round layer cake pan; line the bottom with wax paper, and grease the paper. Preheat the oven to 350 degrees, setting a rack in the center.
2. Sift together the flour, baking powder, and salt into a large mixing bowl. Press the sugar through a wire sieve into the flour mixture. Mix well with a wire whisk; then make a well in the center. Drop in the egg yolks, then add the milk, oil, melted chocolate, and vanilla. Stir briskly with the whisk just long enough to blend.
3. In a small bowl, with electric beaters, beat the egg whites until stiff but not dry. Carefully fold into the chocolate mixture.
4. Pour the batter into the prepared pan. Tap once on the counter to eliminate any large air bubbles. Bake for about 30 minutes, or until a wooden pick comes out clean. Transfer to a wire rack, and allow to cool in the pan.

5. When the cake has cooled, run a sharp knife around the edges to be certain it is loose; then turn out, and carefully remove the paper. Place top side up, on a large round plate or platter (it should have slightly raised edges). Prick the surface of the cake with a two-tined kitchen fork as you would a pie-crust, pricking through to the bottom.

6. Combine the corn syrup and rum in a liquid measuring cup; slowly pour it over the cake so that most is absorbed. Let it stand overnight; after a few hours, spoon some of the excess sauce from the plate over the top, so that it is well saturated. (It will keep well for a day or two.)

7. When ready to serve, prepare the topping as directed, spread it over the top of the cake, and garnish with the chocolate scrolls or shaved semisweet chocolate.

MAKES 8 TO 10 SERVINGS.

SWEETENED WHIPPED CREAM TOPPING

1 cup heavy cream
1 tablespoon sugar
1/2 teaspoon vanilla extract

Whip the cream until slightly thickened; then beat in the sugar and vanilla. Continue beating until almost stiff. Use immediately.

HUNGARIAN CHOCOLATE WALNUT TORTE

A dense one-layer walnut cake and a first cousin to Sachertorte of Viennese origin. The top of the torte is glazed with apricot purée, then thinly iced with chocolate frosting, which is reserved from part of the cake batter. Chopped walnuts pressed around the sides provide an attractive finishing touch.

4 ounces semisweet chocolate, chopped into coarse pieces
5 tablespoons unsalted butter
4 large eggs, separated, at room temperature
6 tablespoons confectioners' sugar, sifted
3/4 cup ground walnuts (page 20)
1/8 teaspoon salt
1/3 to 1/2 cup apricot preserves
1/2 cup coarse-chopped walnuts, for garnish

1. Grease the bottom and sides of an 8-inch springform pan. Dust with flour, and tap out the excess. Preheat the oven to 350 degrees, setting a rack one-third up from the bottom.

2. Place the chocolate and butter in a small, heavy saucepan, and set over very low heat. Stir occasionally with a wire whisk when they begin to melt, then briskly toward the end just long enough so that the mixture is smooth. Set aside briefly.

3. Place the egg yolks and sugar in a medium-size mixing bowl. Stir with a wire whisk until creamy; do not beat. Gradually stir in the warm chocolate mixture. Use the whisk, and again do not beat. Remove 1/2 cup of this mixture, and set aside (it will be used later as frosting). Stir the ground walnuts into the remaining batter.

4. Beat the egg whites and salt with electric beaters until stiff but not dry. Stir at least one-fourth of the whites into the chocolate mixture to lighten it; then carefully fold in the remainder until it is thoroughly blended.

5. Pour the mixture into the springform pan. Bake for about 45 minutes, or until the torte pulls slightly away from the sides of the pan and the top is slightly springy to the touch. Cool the torte in the pan on a rack. When it is completely cool, about 1 hour, release and remove the side of the pan, leaving the torte on the bottom. Slide a sharp, thin knife under the torte to loosen; then, with a wide spatula, transfer it to a cake rack.

6. Heat the apricot preserves in a small saucepan just long enough to thin. Press the mixture through a wire sieve onto the top of the torte, and spread smoothly with the back of a spoon to the edges. Allow to cool for a few minutes, until set.

Note: The pieces of apricot are not used. If the preserves are chunky with fruit, you may need the 1/2 cup; if they are thin, 1/3 cup will be adequate.

7. Using a small spatula, spread the reserved chocolate mixture around the sides of the torte; spread the remainder over the top (it should be thick enough to spread and adhere, yet soft enough so that a minimum of the excess slowly drips off the bottom).

8. Press the chopped walnuts around the sides of the torte and just barely around the top rim. Allow the torte to stand until the frosting is firm; then transfer it to a cake plate. Serve within a few hours, so that the glaze remains shiny.

9. Serve the torte at room temperature, and cut into wedges.

MAKES 6 TO 8 SERVINGS.

CHOCOLATE SIN

This cake is so sinfully rich, so chocolaty, and so easy to make, you will be tempted to bake it often. It is unlike other cakes or tortes in that it has the smooth consistency of cheesecake.

8 ounces dark sweet chocolate, chopped into coarse pieces
1 tablespoon water
3/4 cup (1 1/2 sticks) unsalted butter, softened
1 tablespoon sugar
1 tablespoon cornstarch
4 large eggs, separated, at room temperature
1/4 teaspoon salt
Whipped Cream Topping (recipe follows)
1/2 to 1 square unsweetened chocolate, for garnish

1. Grease only the bottom, not the sides, of an 8-inch springform pan. Preheat the oven to 350 degrees, setting a rack in the center.

2. Melt the dark sweet chocolate with the water in a small, heavy saucepan set over very low heat, stirring occasionally until mixture is melted and smooth; remove and set aside.

3. In a mixing bowl, with a wire whisk, whip the butter (it should be almost meltingly soft) along with the sugar and cornstarch. When the mixture is blended, add the egg yolks, and continue to whisk until creamy; do not beat. Add the chocolate, and stir with the whisk until well blended.

4. In a separate bowl beat the egg whites with the salt until stiff but still moist. Whisk about one-fourth of the egg whites into the chocolate mixture to lighten it; then gently whisk in the remainder, using a light folding action.

5. Pour the batter into the prepared springform pan; shake lightly to settle. Bake for 15 minutes. Turn off the oven heat, and leaving the oven door slightly opened (about 4 inches), allow the cake to cool for 10 minutes.

6. Remove the pan from the oven, and place it on a wire rack to cool. As the cake begins to draw away from the sides of the pan, run a knife around the edges so that it pulls away evenly. Allow to cool to room temperature; then release the sides of the springform.

Note: As the cake cools, it will sink in the center, leaving a thin rim of firm cake around the edge; the center will be soft.

7. When ready to serve, prepare the topping as directed, and spread it over the top of the cake. Using a vegetable peeler, scrape the sides of the unsweetened chocolate square directly onto the whipped cream to cover it generously. Cut the cake into wedges.

Note: This cake is especially delicious when served slightly warm. Whip the cream lightly, and spoon it over the cut portions; garnish with the chocolate shavings.

MAKES 6 TO 8 SERVINGS.

WHIPPED CREAM TOPPING

1 cup heavy cream
3 tablespoons confectioners' sugar
1 teaspoon vanilla extract

Whip the cream, sugar, and vanilla until stiff and spreadable. Do not overwhip, or the cream will become buttery.

LE GÂTEAU VICTOIRE

This is a tender chocolaty dessert confection made with a chocolate crumb crust bottom. When served soon after it has cooled, it has a gossamer texture. When held overnight, it is more like velvety cheesecake. Either way, it is delicious.

CHOCOLATE CRUMB CRUST

1 cup chocolate wafer crumbs
1/4 cup (1/2 stick) unsalted butter, melted

CHOCOLATE BATTER

6 ounces semisweet chocolate, chopped into coarse pieces
3/4 cup (1 1/2 sticks) butter, cut into chunks
3/4 cup sugar
6 eggs, separated, at room temperature
1 tablespoon grated rind from 1 orange
1/4 teaspoon salt
Whipped Cream Topping (recipe follows)
Candied Orange Peel (page 18), for garnish

1. *For the crust:* Grease the bottom of a 9-inch springform pan. Combine the wafer crumbs and melted butter; press onto the pan bottom firmly and evenly. Grease the sides of the pan, and attach. Preheat the oven to 325 degrees, setting a rack in the center.

2. *For the batter:* Combine the chocolate, butter, and sugar in the top of a double boiler. Set over barely simmering water, and stir occasionally until the chocolate is melted and blended smoothly with the butter and sugar. Remove from the heat, and turn into a large mixing bowl; cool slightly; then add the egg yolks, and beat just until incorporated. Stir in the grated orange rind.

In the large bowl of an electric mixer, beat the egg whites with the salt until soft peaks form. They should be firm but not dry. Stir about one-third of the egg whites into the chocolate mixture to lighten it. Fold in the remainder, lightly but thoroughly so that no white traces remain.

3. Turn the batter into the prepared pan, and lightly tap it two or three times on the counter to eliminate any large air bubbles. Bake for about 40 minutes, or until a thin crisp crust forms on the top and has crackled. The cake will quiver when lightly shaken. Remove from the oven, and place on a rack. Release the sides by running a sharp knife cleanly around the edges, leaving the pan sides attached. Before serving, allow to cool for at least 1 hour, when it is just barely at room temperature; or cool completely, but serve within 6 to 8 hours to preserve the gossamer texture.

Note: As the cake cools, it will sink, forming a high irregular edge, which will be filled with whipped cream before serving. Although the cake is best served the same day it is prepared, it is also delicious but denser if held overnight, or even several days. Do not refrigerate, but cover loosely with foil.

4. When ready to serve, prepare the topping, and spread it over the top of the crust to the edges. Garnish with the candied orange peel. Remove the sides from the pan, and cut into wedges.

MAKES 10 OR MORE SERVINGS.

WHIPPED CREAM TOPPING

1 cup heavy cream
2 tablespoons confectioners' sugar
3/4 teaspoon vanilla extract

Pour the cream into a chilled mixing bowl; add the sugar and vanilla. Beat with chilled beaters until the cream is thickened and spreadable (do not overbeat, or the cream will become buttery).

CHOCOLATE CREAM CAKE DELUXE

This cake—or should it be called a baked dessert?—is as sensational as it is unusual: exceptionally creamy and bittersweet chocolaty and surprisingly baked in a chocolate crumb crust.

CHOCOLATE CRUMB CRUST

2 cups chocolate wafer crumbs
1/2 cup (1 stick) unsalted butter, melted

CHOCOLATE CREAM FILLING

1 cup heavy cream
16 ounces semisweet chocolate, chopped into coarse pieces
8 large eggs, separated, at room temperature
2 teaspoons vanilla extract
1/2 cup sifted all-purpose flour
1/2 teaspoon salt
Sweetened Whipped Cream (recipe follows)

1. *For the crust:* Grease the bottom and halfway up the sides of a 10-inch springform pan.

In a small bowl combine the wafer crumbs with the melted butter, using a fork to distribute the butter evenly. Transfer to the prepared pan. Using your fingertips or a spoon, press the crumbs evenly and firmly on the bottom and halfway up the sides. The mixture should be a little thicker where the bottom and sides meet. Set aside while preparing the filling. Do not refrigerate.

2. *For the filling:* Preheat the oven to 350 degrees, setting a rack one-third up from the bottom.

Combine the cream and chocolate in the top of a double boiler. Set over barely simmering water, and stir occasionally until the chocolate is melted and blended with the cream. Set aside to cool until tepid.

In a large mixing bowl, using a wire whisk, briefly beat the egg yolks with the vanilla just until light. Gradually whisk in the flour, mixing only until it is incorporated. Add the cooled chocolate mixture, stirring briskly with the whisk until it is evenly blended.

In the large bowl of an electric mixer beat the egg whites with the salt until soft peaks form. They should be firm but not dry. Using the whisk, stir about one-third of the egg whites into the chocolate mixture to lighten it. Fold in the remainder, lightly but thoroughly so that no white traces remain.

3. Pour the batter into the prepared pan, and shake it slightly to level. Bake in the preheated oven for 30 minutes. At this point the outer third of the cake should look baked and feel springy to the touch, but the center should be soft and quiver slightly when the pan is shaken. (If the center seems excessively soft, bake for a few minutes longer.)

4. Remove the pan to a rack, and allow the cake to cool completely, until the center is firm enough for smooth cutting. This may take as long as 8 hours. If preferred, let it stand overnight, covered with plastic wrap. Do not refrigerate.

5. To serve, remove the sides of the springform pan. The cake will have pulled away from the sides, leaving the crust intact. Cut into wedges with a knife rinsed in hot water. Serve each wedge on a dessert plate with a large spoonful of the whipped cream alongside.

MAKES 12 TO 16 SERVINGS.

SWEETENED WHIPPED CREAM

2 cups heavy cream
1/4 cup confectioners' sugar
1 1/2 teaspoons vanilla extract

Pour the cream into a chilled mixing bowl. Press the sugar through a wire sieve into the cream. Add the vanilla. Beat with chilled beaters until the cream mounds softly, not until stiff. Serve immediately.

Note: The cream may be whipped in advance and refrigerated. If it has begun to separate, beat it briefly with a wire whisk before using.

GALETTE AU CHOCOLAT

Rich, dense, thin, and chocolaty—a masterpiece of French simplicity.

1 tablespoon fine dry breadcrumbs
1 tablespoon plus 1 1/2 teaspoons unsweetened cocoa powder
1/2 cup (1 stick) unsalted butter, softened
1 1/3 cups granulated sugar
3 large eggs, separated, at room temperature
3 ounces unsweetened chocolate, melted and cooled
1 teaspoon vanilla extract
1 cup ground walnuts (page 20)
6 tablespoons sifted all-purpose flour
1/4 teaspoon salt
Confectioners' sugar and 1 candied red cherry, for garnish
Crème Chantilly (recipe follows)

1. Grease the bottom and about 2 inches up the sides of a 9-inch springform pan. Combine the breadcrumbs with the 1 1/2 teaspoons cocoa. Pour into the greased pan, tilting and turning the pan to cover the greased areas; tap out the excess.

2. Preheat the oven to 325 degrees, placing a rack in the lower third of the oven.

3. In a mixing bowl, with electric beaters, cream the butter; then gradually add the sugar, and continue beating until well blended. Beat in the egg yolks, one at a time, beating well after each addition to incorporate thoroughly. Blend in the melted chocolate and vanilla. Combine the walnuts, flour, and remaining 1 tablespoon cocoa; add to the chocolate mixture, and beat on low speed just long enough to combine.

4. In a separate mixing bowl beat the egg whites with the salt until they hold a definite peak, not until stiff or dry. Gently fold them into the chocolate mixture; then turn the batter into the prepared pan, spreading it evenly.

5. Bake for about 35 minutes, or until a wooden pick in-

serted in the center comes out clean. Cool the torte in the pan on a rack. The batter will rise as it bakes, then pull away from the sides of the pan and fall as it cools so that the cake will be only about an inch high.

6. When the torte is cooled, remove the sides of the pan; loosen the bottom with a thin spatula. Dust the top heavily with confectioners' sugar put through a wire sieve; then transfer to a serving platter. Garnish the center with a single candied cherry.

7. When ready to serve, prepare the Crème Chantilly as directed. Cut the torte into wedges, and place each wedge on a dessert plate with a spoonful of the whipped cream alongside.

MAKES 8 OR MORE SERVINGS.

CRÈME CHANTILLY

1 cup heavy cream
1 tablespoon confectioners' sugar
1/2 teaspoon vanilla extract

Whip the cream with the sugar and vanilla until it barely holds a shape. It should be soft, very soft, not at all firm.

Note: To prepare in advance, whip the cream and refrigerate it, but for no longer than an hour or so. If the cream begins to separate, beat it lightly with a wire whisk to restore the original soft-whipped quality.

CURRANT CHOCOLATE WHISKY CAKE

An exceptionally moist and chocolaty cake with a handsome marble glaze. The cake is best when made at least a day in advance, but it improves in flavor if it is kept several days before being glazed. The currants, ground almonds, and whisky contribute to its long-keeping quality.

1/4 cup currants
1/4 cup Scotch whisky
8 ounces dark sweet chocolate, chopped into coarse pieces
3 tablespoons strong coffee
1/2 cup (1 stick) unsalted butter
3 eggs, separated, at room temperature
2/3 cup sugar
1/4 cup sifted all-purpose flour
1 cup (about 2/3 cup whole) fine-ground blanched almonds
   (page 20)
Scant 1/4 teaspoon salt
Bittersweet Chocolate Glaze (recipe follows)

1. Grease a 9 × 1 1/2-inch-round layer cake pan. Line the bottom with wax paper; grease the paper, and dust with flour, tapping out the excess. Preheat the oven to 375 degrees, setting a rack in the center.

2. Place the currants and whisky in a small bowl, and set aside while preparing the cake batter.

3. Melt the chocolate with the coffee in the top of a double boiler set over barely simmering water, stirring until smooth; then remove from the heat. Stir in the butter, a chunk at a time, blending thoroughly before each chunk is added. Set aside.

4. In a large mixing bowl, with electric beaters, beat the egg yolks with the sugar until pale and creamy. Stir in the chocolate mixture.

5. Combine the flour and ground almonds; stir into the chocolate mixture. Then stir in the currants and whisky, just long enough to blend thoroughly.

6. Whip the egg whites with the salt until they are stiff but not dry. Stir about one-third into the chocolate mixture to lighten it; then fold in the remainder.

7. Pour the cake batter into the prepared pan, and bake for 20 minutes (about 1 1/2 inches of the outside edges should be firm, but the center should be soft and seemingly unbaked). Cool on a rack for 10 minutes; loosen the sides, and turn out onto a rack to cool completely, leaving the wax paper intact.

Note: For best flavor, wrap and store the torte at room temperature overnight (or for several days, if desired) before adding the glaze.

8. When ready to apply the glaze, carefully remove the wax paper, and place the cake on the rack over a sheet of wax paper (to catch any drippings). Then prepare the chocolate glaze as directed. When it has cooled to the proper consistency, pour it onto the center of the cake. Spread it smoothly and evenly to the edges, letting a little dribble down the sides; then spread it around the sides so that it covers them thinly. Set aside in a cool place to firm the glaze before serving. Then cut into wedges.

Note: The glaze will hold its shine until ready to serve, overnight if desired, and when kept at room temperature.

MAKES 8 SERVINGS.

BITTERSWEET CHOCOLATE GLAZE

2 ounces unsweetened chocolate, chopped into coarse pieces
2 ounces semisweet chocolate, chopped into coarse pieces
1/4 cup (1/2 stick) unsalted butter, softened
2 teaspoons white corn syrup

Combine the two chocolates, butter, and corn syrup in the top of a double boiler. Melt over hot water, stirring to blend. Remove from the heat, and beat with a wooden spoon until cool and slightly thickened (almost set but still pourable). Use immediately.

BELGIAN CHOCOLATE CAKE

A rich chocolate and almond cake from the French, not the Flemish, part of Belgium. It is served unfrosted with a simple accompaniment of lightly whipped and sweetened cream.

8 ounces semisweet chocolate, chopped into coarse pieces
2 teaspoons instant espresso, dissolved in 1/2 cup hot water
1/2 cup sugar
1/4 teaspoon salt
3 tablespoons cold unsalted butter, cut into 4 or 5 chunks
4 large-egg yolks, at room temperature
1 teaspoon vanilla extract
1/2 cup cornstarch
1 cup chopped, toasted, blanched almonds (page 20)
6 large-egg whites, at room temperature
Cream Chantilly (recipe follows)

1. Grease an 8-inch springform pan; then dust with fine dry breadcrumbs. Preheat the oven to 325 degrees, setting a rack one-third up from the bottom.

2. Place the chocolate and coffee in a large heatproof mixing bowl. Set over a saucepan of simmering water. Heat, stirring, until the chocolate is melted and blended with the coffee. Add the sugar and salt, and stir until dissolved. Remove the bowl from over the water; then stir in the butter until blended.

3. Using a wire whisk, beat in the egg yolks, one at a time, beating well after each addition. Stir in the vanilla. Sift the cornstarch over the top of the batter, and mix until smooth. Stir in the almonds.

4. In a separate bowl beat the egg whites until they stand in soft peaks. Fold them into the chocolate batter, gently but thoroughly, in three additions.

5. Pour the batter into the prepared pan. Tap it on the counter two or three times to release any large air bubbles. Bake

for 45 to 50 minutes, or until a wooden pick inserted 1 inch from the center comes out clean. (Do not overbake; the center will firm as the cake cools.) Place the pan on a rack, and cool to room temperature before cutting and serving. (If preferred, and for best flavor, let it stand overnight, covered with plastic wrap. Do not refrigerate.)

6. To serve, cut into wedges, and place each on a dessert plate with a large spoonful of the whipped cream alongside.

Note: A crust will form on the top of the cake as it bakes, which will wrinkle as it cools and soften when it is covered and stored.

MAKES 8 SERVINGS.

CREAM CHANTILLY

> 1 1/2 *cups heavy cream*
> 3 *tablespoons confectioners' sugar*
> 3/4 *teaspoon vanilla extract*

Whip the cream with the sugar and vanilla until it mounds lightly, not until stiff. It should be somewhat sauce-like. Serve immediately.

VIENNESE CHOCOLATE ALMOND TORTE

A typical Austrian torte; rich with nuts, dense and moist, and thinly covered with a beautiful glossy chocolate glaze.

1 cup (2 sticks) unsalted butter, softened
1 cup confectioners' sugar, sifted
1 teaspoon vanilla extract
6 large eggs, separated, at room temperature
4 ounces semisweet chocolate, grated (page 9)
1 cup (4 ounces) ground, blanched almonds (page 20)
2/3 cup fine dry breadcrumbs
1/4 teaspoon salt
Bittersweet Chocolate Glaze (recipe follows)
12 blanched almonds, for garnish

1. Grease the bottom and halfway up the sides of a 9-inch springform pan. Dust with fine dry breadcrumbs; tap out the excess. Preheat the oven to 375 degrees, setting the rack one-third up from the bottom.

2. In the bowl of an electric mixer cream the butter. Add the sugar, and beat until light and fluffy. Blend in the vanilla. Add the egg yolks, two at a time, beating until thoroughly incorporated after each addition.

3. Using a rubber spatula, blend in the grated chocolate, ground almonds, and breadcrumbs in that order, mixing just long enough after each addition to incorporate.

4. In a separate mixer bowl beat the egg whites with the salt until they hold a definite peak, not until stiff and dry. Stir one-third of the egg whites into the chocolate mixture to lighten it; then fold in the remainder until no white traces remain.

5. Turn the mixture into the prepared pan, taking care to spread it as level as possible. Bake for about 35 minutes, or until the top is evenly browned and firm in the center to the touch. Place on a rack to cool for 10 minutes; then release and

remove the sides of the pan, and allow to cool completely. (The torte will have risen only slightly and will be about an inch or so high.)

6. Prepare the chocolate glaze as directed. Place the cooled cake and rack on a tray covered with a sheet of wax paper to catch the drippings. Pour the glaze onto the center top of the cake. Spread smoothly and evenly with a metal spatula to the edges, letting a little dribble down the sides; then spread so that it covers them thinly.

7. Before the glaze has set, arrange the blanched almonds in a circle around the top edge, spacing them so that there is one for each serving. Set the torte aside in a cool place for at least 1 1/2 hours, or until the glaze has set; then transfer to a serving plate. Do not refrigerate or let the torte stand for more than a few hours, or the glaze will lose its beautiful shine.

MAKES 12 SERVINGS.

BITTERSWEET CHOCOLATE GLAZE

1/2 cup heavy cream
8 ounces semisweet chocolate, chopped into coarse pieces

Pour the cream into a medium-size, heavy saucepan; add the chopped chocolate. Place over medium-low heat, and stir with a spoon until the chocolate begins to melt and is partially blended with the cream. Continue stirring with a wire whisk until the mixture is well blended and smooth. Remove from the heat, and place the pan in a bowl of cold water to hasten the cooling process. Let stand, stirring occasionally, for about 15 minutes or so, or until the mixture has a spreading consistency but is still pourable.

Note: Although a wire whisk is used to blend the cream and chocolate smoothly, the mixture should not be stirred so vigorously that any air is incorporated. It must be thin and smooth, so that it is pourable.

BAVARIAN CHOCOLATE PECAN TORTE

An unusual two-layer torte. The base, made with ground nuts and zwieback crumbs, is moist and dense. The topping is a chocolate Bavarian cream with chopped pecans and marshmallow bits.

TORTE LAYER

3 eggs
1 cup sugar
1 cup pecans, chopped into fine pieces
1 cup fine zwieback crumbs*
1 teaspoon baking powder
1/4 teaspoon salt
1/2 teaspoon ground cinnamon

CHOCOLATE LAYER

1 1/4 teaspoons unflavored gelatin
1/4 cup cold water
4 tablespoons sugar
1/4 teaspoon salt
1 cup heavy cream
1 egg, separated
1 ounce unsweetened chocolate, grated (page 9)
6 large marshmallows, cut into small pieces
1/2 cup chopped pecans
1-ounce-square unsweetened chocolate, for garnish

*Zwieback (often known as Holland rusks) is a crisp dry bread, which is made with a minimum amount of sugar and spices. The brand used here is Nabisco, which is available in most supermarkets. (Half the 6-ounce package—12 pieces—will yield the 1 cup crumbs required.)

1. *For the torte layer:* Grease well a 9-inch springform pan. Preheat the oven to 325 degrees, setting a rack in the center.

In a large mixer bowl, with electric beaters, beat the eggs until foamy. Gradually add the sugar while beating, and continue beating until the mixture is thick and creamy.

Combine the pecans, zwieback crumbs, baking powder, salt, and cinnamon; blend well. Gradually fold into the egg mixture, gently but completely.

Pour the mixture into the springform pan. Tap it lightly on the counter to eliminate any large air bubbles. Bake for 40 minutes, or until the cake begins to pull away slightly from the sides of the pan. Set the pan on a rack to cool completely.

Note: As the torte bakes, it will form a thin crust, which will crack as it cools, and will have a thin, high rim at the edges.

2. *For the chocolate layer:* Combine the gelatin, water, 2 tablespoons of the sugar, and salt in the top of a double boiler. Stir; then let stand for a few minutes until the gelatin has softened. Stir in 3/4 cup of the cream. Cook over hot water until the gelatin has dissolved.

Beat the egg yolk slightly in a small bowl. Stir a little of the hot cream mixture into the egg yolk; then return to the double boiler. Add the grated chocolate. Cook, stirring, until the mixture thickens slightly and the chocolate has blended smoothly with the custard mixture. (Do not overcook, or the custard will curdle.)

Remove the custard from the heat, pour into a mixing bowl, and chill, stirring occasionally, until it mounds slightly when dropped from a spoon.

Beat the egg white until soft peaks form; then gradually beat in the remaining 2 tablespoons sugar. Continue beating until stiff and glossy. Fold into the gelatin mixture.

Using the same bowl and beaters for the egg white (without rinsing), whip the remaining 1/4 cup cream until it mounds softly. Fold it into the gelatin mixture; then fold in the marshmallows and pecans.

3. Spoon the mixture over the torte layer, spreading it evenly to the edges, so that only a thin rim of the torte shows.

4. Using a vegetable peeler, grate half the square of chocolate over the top of the torte. Cover the pan with aluminum foil, and refrigerate until the chocolate layer is set. Remove from the refrigerator 20 minutes before serving.

5. To serve, run a sharp knife around the sides of the torte, then remove the sides of the springform pan, and cut into wedges.

Note: The torte has better flavor if made a day in advance.

MAKES 10 OR MORE SERVINGS.

CHOCOLATE ALMOND MOUSSE TORTE

A torte in a class by itself. The batter, a rich mousse, makes the layers and filling. The resulting torte is only about an inch and a half high and has an intriguing slightly chewy and sandy texture.

1/2 cup (1 stick) unsalted butter, softened
1/2 teaspoon vanilla extract
1 1/4 cups superfine sugar
4 ounces unsweetened chocolate, chopped into coarse pieces
3 eggs, separated, at room temperature
1 cup ground toasted almonds (page 20)
1/8 teaspoon salt
Confectioners' sugar, for garnish

1. Grease well and flour two 8-inch layer cake pans. Preheat the oven to 350 degrees, setting a rack in the middle.

2. Cream the butter and vanilla in a large mixing bowl, using a wooden spoon. Gradually mix in the superfine sugar.

3. Melt the chocolate in a small saucepan set over very low heat. When it is melted, immediately blend it into the butter mixture. Stir in first the egg yolks, then the ground almonds, mixing until well blended.

4. Beat the egg whites with the salt until stiff but not dry. Stir a few spoonfuls into the chocolate mixture; then fold in the remainder until no white traces remain.

5. Remove 1 cup of the mixture, and set aside at room temperature to use as filling. Divide the remaining batter equally between the two pans (about 1 cup each), and spread it evenly. It will cover the bottoms thinly.

6. Bake the layers for about 20 minutes, or until the tops just feel slightly springy to the touch. Invert immediately onto racks lined with wax paper, and allow to cool. The layers will be only about 1/2 inch high.

7. Place one of the inverted cake layers on a flat serving

plate. Spread the top with the reserved chocolate mousse. Set
the second inverted layer over the filling. Sift the confectioners'
sugar over the top layer. Let stand, covered with an inverted
bowl, at room temperature until ready to serve, but no more
than 6 hours. (If it is held longer, refrigerate or freeze it, but
bring it to room temperature before serving.)

Note: For an especially attractive presentation, place a paper doily over the top of the cake before sifting on the confectioners' sugar. Remove the doily carefully, so that the design is
intact.

MAKES 6 TO 8 SERVINGS.

V
COLD DESSERTS

CHOCOLATE POTS DE CRÈME
BITTERSWEET CHOCOLATE PUDDING
EVIL SPIRITS
CHOCOLATE CREAM GRAND MARNIER
BITTERSWEET CHOCOLATE CREAM
CHOCOLATE CRÈME DE LA CRÈME
COLETTES
LEMON FOAM IN CHOCOLATE CUPS
BUDINO DI RICOTTA
CHOCOLATE ALMOND MARQUISE
THE CHOCOLATE MARQUISE
CHOCOLATE INNOCENCE
COLD CHOCOLATE SOUFFLÉ WITH RUM CUSTARD
CHOCOLATE MACAROON ICEBOX TORTE
TURINOIS
FRENCH CHOCOLATE FONDANT
MARZIPAN TORTE
DACQUOISE AU CHOCOLAT
MILK CHOCOLATE BAVARIAN

CHOCOLATE CHRISTMAS PUDDING
GÂTEAU MOULE AU CHOCOLAT
CASSIS WHITE CHOCOLATE CHEESECAKE
CHOCOLATE IN CHOCOLATE CHEESECAKE
ALMOND MARBLE CHEESECAKE

CHOCOLATE POTS DE CRÈME

The very best pots de crème, a French creation, are made with egg yolks and cream. They are served au naturel, *in tiny porcelain cups with lids, the creamy mixture filling the tiny cups to the brim.*

4 ounces semisweet chocolate
1 cup heavy cream
3 egg yolks, at room temperature
1/4 cup crème de cacao, a chocolate-flavored liqueur

1. Chop or break the chocolate into small pieces, and place in a small, heavy saucepan with the cream. Set over medium heat, and stir occasionally until the chocolate is melted and the cream comes to a full boil. Reduce the heat, and simmer, stirring, for 3 minutes.

2. In a small mixing bowl stir the egg yolks with a wire whisk just to mix. While stirring, gradually pour in the hot chocolate mixture in a steady stream. Do not beat. When the mixture is well blended, stir in the crème de cacao.

3. Strain the mixture into a 4-cup liquid measuring container; then carefully pour into four pots de crème cups, demitasse cups, or ramekins with a 4-ounce capacity. Tap the cups lightly on the counter to eliminate air bubbles. Cover the pots de crème cups with their lids, the other containers with plastic wrap. When they are cool, place them in the refrigerator to chill before serving.

MAKES 4 SERVINGS.

BITTERSWEET CHOCOLATE PUDDING

A simple chocolate pudding made from pure ingredients—infinitely better than any prepared from a package mix.

> 2 ounces unsweetened chocolate
> 2 cups milk
> 1/2 cup sugar
> 2 tablespoons cornstarch
> 1/4 teaspoon salt
> 1 egg, at room temperature
> 1 teaspoon vanilla extract

1. Chop the chocolate into small, coarse pieces. Place in a heavy saucepan, and add the milk. Heat gradually, allowing the chocolate to melt slowly. (It will appear grainy, but will smooth out in the finished pudding.)

2. Combine the sugar, cornstarch, salt, and egg. Gradually stir in the hot milk mixture. Return to the saucepan, and cook over low heat, stirring until smooth. Boil for 1 minute, stirring. Remove the pan from the heat; cool slightly; then stir in the vanilla.

3. Pour the pudding into small dessert bowls. Cover each with a layer of plastic wrap to prevent a skin from forming. Refrigerate them until well chilled.

MAKES 4 SERVINGS.

EVIL SPIRITS

A classic recipe for chocolate mousse—bittersweet and dense, almost like a solid morsel of chocolate. It is served in small portions in pots de crème or demitasse cups. The crème de cacao heightens the flavor and gives it a "spirited" lift.

6 ounces semisweet chocolate, chopped into coarse pieces
6 large eggs, separated, at room temperature
1 tablespoon crème de cacao, a chocolate-flavored liqueur
1/8 teaspoon salt

1. Melt the chocolate in the top of a double boiler set over barely simmering water. Remove from the heat, stir to smooth, and set aside to cool slightly.

2. Beat the egg yolks with electric beaters until pale and thickened (when the beaters are lifted, the mixture should fall back in a ribbon). Stir in the cooled melted chocolate and crème de cacao.

3. Beat the egg whites until foamy; add the salt and beat until stiff but not dry. Stir about one-third of the egg whites into the chocolate mixture to lighten it; then fold in the remainder until no white traces remain.

4. Spoon the mousse into pots de crème cups or demitasse cups. Cover with pots de crème lids or with plastic wrap. Chill well before serving, at least 6 hours or overnight, if preferred.

5. To serve, place the cups of mousse on their saucers with demitasse spoons on the side. Do not garnish, since anything, even whipped cream, interferes with the velvety texture.

MAKES 8 SERVINGS.

CHOCOLATE CREAM GRAND MARNIER

An orange-flavored chocolate mousse attractively served in wine goblets.

6 ounces semisweet chocolate, chopped into coarse pieces
6 tablespoons strong coffee
1/4 cup Grand Marnier or other orange-flavored liqueur
1/4 cup sugar
2 cups heavy cream
1/2 teaspoon vanilla extract
Candied Orange Peel (page 18) or chocolate scrolls
    (page 11)

1. Combine the chocolate, coffee, and liqueur in the top of a double boiler. Place over simmering water, and stir until the chocolate is melted and blended. Add the sugar, and continue to stir until very smooth and glossy. Remove from the heat, and refrigerate until cooled.

2. Whip the cream with the vanilla until thick but not buttery. Using a wire whisk, gradually blend in the cooled chocolate mixture. Mix lightly and just long enough so that the mixture is of one color.

3. Spoon the mousse into six individual glasses, preferably wine goblets. Cover the tops with plastic wrap, and refrigerate until ready to serve—several hours or overnight.

4. When ready to serve, top each serving with a few orange peels or chocolate scrolls.

MAKES 6 SERVINGS.

BITTERSWEET CHOCOLATE CREAM

An easily made last-minute dessert for four which requires a minimum amount of chilling before serving.

6 ounces semisweet chocolate, chopped into coarse pieces
1/4 cup (1/2 stick) unsalted butter
1 egg yolk
1 cup heavy cream
1/4 cup superfine sugar

1. Combine the chocolate and butter in a small, heavy saucecepan. Set over low heat, and stir occasionally just until the chocolate is melted and is blended with the butter. Remove from the heat, and set aside until tepid. Then add the egg yolk, beating with a wire whisk until thoroughly incorporated.

2. In a large mixing bowl whip the cream until it begins to thicken; then gradually beat in the sugar, and continue beating until stiff.

3. Stir a little of the whipped cream into the chocolate mixture to lighten it; then fold into the remaining whipped cream. Turn the mixture into four individual soufflé dishes or other containers with a 6-ounce capacity. Refrigerate for at least 30 minutes to firm, or longer, if desired. Serve without garnish.

MAKES 4 SERVINGS.

CHOCOLATE CRÈME DE LA CRÈME

Neither a mousse nor a Bavarian—no eggs are required—but just as special and easier to make. This airy dessert is almost pure whipped cream, lightly flavored with chocolate and vanilla.

1 envelope unflavored gelatin
1/3 cup cold water
2 ounces unsweetened chocolate, chopped into coarse pieces
1/2 cup confectioners' sugar
1 cup milk
3/4 cup granulated sugar
1/4 teaspoon salt
2 teaspoons vanilla extract
2 cups heavy cream
Chocolate scrolls (page 11) or chocolate sprinkles (page 13)

1. Sprinkle the gelatin over the cold water; set aside to soften.

2. Combine the chocolate, confectioners' sugar, and milk in a 1 1/2-quart heavy saucepan. Set over moderate heat; cook, stirring occasionally with a wire whisk, until the chocolate has melted and the mixture comes just to a boil, thickens slightly, and is smooth. Remove from the heat, and add the softened gelatin, granulated sugar, and salt. Stir with the whisk until all have dissolved; then blend in the vanilla. Set aside.

3. Whip the cream until it holds a semifirm shape, not until stiff. Refrigerate.

4. Place the bowl of chocolate mixture in a larger bowl partly filled with ice and cold water. Stir frequently with the whisk until the mixture thickens to the consistency of a medium cream sauce and feels cool to the touch. Watch carefully toward the end, for it will thicken quickly.

5. When the chocolate mixture is ready, fold in the chilled whipped cream with the whisk. When it is blended,

pour it into a glass bowl, preferably one with a stem (it should have at least a 6-cup capacity because there will be five cups of the chocolate cream). Cover the top with plastic wrap or foil, and refrigerate for several hours until set or overnight.

6. When ready to serve, garnish the top lightly with the chocolate scrolls or sprinkles. Spoon out in mounds onto dessert plates or into dessert dishes.

MAKES 6 TO 8 SERVINGS.

COLETTES

Snowy chiffon cream served in individual fluted chocolate cups, each topped with crushed almond praline and a cherry. A special confection. The cups are surprisingly easy to make and are not as fragile as they look.

9 Chocolate Cups (recipe follows)
2 teaspoons unflavored gelatin
3 tablespoons cold water
12 tablespoons sugar
3 tablespoons flour, sifted
Scant 1/2 teaspoon salt
1 1/8 cups milk
1/2 teaspoon vanilla extract
1/4 teaspoon almond extract
2/3 cup heavy cream
2 large-egg whites, at room temperature
1/4 teaspoon cream of tartar
About 1/3 cup Almond Praline (page 19), crushed, for
    garnish
9 maraschino cherries with stems, for garnish

1. Prepare the chocolate cups as directed, and refrigerate.

2. Sprinkle the gelatin over the cold water to soften; set aside.

3. Mix together 6 tablespoons of the sugar, flour, and salt in a heavy saucepan. Gradually stir in the milk. Cook over low heat, stirring, until the mixture comes to a boil.

Remove from the heat, and stir in the softened gelatin. Boil for 1 minute. Pour the mixture into a large mixing bowl and chill, occasionally stirring with a wire whisk, until the mixture is cool and mounds lightly. Beat with the whisk until smooth. Blend in the vanilla and almond extracts.

4. Whip the cream until it mounds lightly. Fold into the gelatin mixture.

5. Beat the egg whites until foamy. Add the cream of tartar, and beat until soft peaks form. Gradually beat in the remaining 6 tablespoons sugar; continue beating to a stiff meringue. Fold the meringue into the gelatin mixture.

6. Spoon the filling into the cups, mounding it well above the tops. Refrigerate until set. Take the chilled cups out of the refrigerator 15 minutes before serving.

7. Just before serving, sprinkle the tops with the crushed praline, and garnish each with a well-drained and dried maraschino cherry.

MAKES 9 COLETTES.

CHOCOLATE CUPS

9 foil 2 1/2-inch cupcake liners*
1 cup (6 ounces) semisweet chocolate morsels
1 tablespoon vegetable shortening

1. Have ready a standard-size muffin tin which will accommodate the 9 cups. Fan out the edges of the foil liners slightly, so that the chocolate coating can be applied evenly.

2. Place the chocolate morsels and shortening in a small (about 2-cup), heavy saucepan. Melt over very low heat, stirring, until the chocolate is melted and is smooth. Remove the pan from the heat, and cool it slightly, just long enough so that you can comfortably hold in your hand one of the liners that contains a spoonful of the chocolate.

3. To coat the liners with chocolate, place 1 measuring tablespoonful of the chocolate in the bottom of one foil liner. Holding it in the palm of your hand and using a small teaspoon, rotate the liner gently while you push and spread the chocolate up the sides to the edges to coat them evenly. (The sides will be thinner than the bottom, which should be heavily

*Foil cupcake liners are readily available in most supermarkets.

coated so that it is firm when chilled.) Place the cup in the muffin tin. Repeat the procedure with the remaining liners and chocolate. Check over carefully, and patch any areas which seem thin with any remaining chocolate.

4. Refrigerate the cups for at least 1 hour, or until they are firm.

5. To unmold, insert the tip of a small pointed knife into the foil on the bottom of one cup to release a small flap; then peel the foil away from the bottom, using your fingers. Pull a strip down the side; then peel the foil away from the sides (it should come away in one long strip). Return the cup to the muffin tin. Repeat with the remaining cups. Refrigerate until ready to use.

Note: The procedure seems complicated, but it is easy, and the chocolate cups are not as fragile as you might think.

MAKES 9 CHOCOLATE CUPS.

LEMON FOAM IN CHOCOLATE CUPS

A creamy lemon-flavored meringue with a candied lemon peel garnish.

> *6 Chocolate Cups (page 113)*
> *1 large-egg white, at room temperature*
> *Scant 1/8 teaspoon salt*
> *6 tablespoons (generous 1/3 cup) light corn syrup*
> *1 tablespoon fresh lemon juice*
> *Candied Lemon Peel (page 18)*

1. Prepare the chocolate cups as directed, and refrigerate. Only six are required.

2. In a small mixing bowl, with electric beaters, beat the egg white with the salt. Beat until stiff but not dry.

3. Heat the corn syrup in a small saucepan until bubbles appear around the edge. While beating, slowly pour the hot syrup into the egg white. Then continue beating until the mixture is stiff and the meringue hangs in peaks from the beaters. Fold in the lemon juice.

4. Spoon the mixture into the cups, and serve immediately or refrigerate until ready to serve, up to 2 hours.

5. To serve, garnish each filled cup with 2 or 3 pieces of the lemon peel.

MAKES 6 SERVINGS.

BUDINO DI RICOTTA

Individual cold puddings made with ricotta cheese, chopped chocolate, and orange rind. An unusual light dessert, especially suitable to end an Italian meal.

> *1 container (15 1/2 ounces) whole milk ricotta*
> *1 large orange with a thick, well-colored skin*
> *3 ounces semisweet chocolate*
> *1/2 cup confectioners' sugar*
> *2 tablespoons light rum*

1. Turn the ricotta into a mixing bowl; set aside.

2. Using a vegetable peeler, strip the zest (orange part only) from half the orange. Chop into fine pieces with a chef's knife; there should be 1 generous tablespoon. Reserve about 1 teaspoon for garnish, and add the rest to the ricotta.

3. Using a chef's knife, chop the chocolate into fine pieces, the largest no more than 1/4 inch; reserve about 2 teaspoons for garnish, and add the remainder to the ricotta.

4. Add the sugar and rum to the ricotta; blend the ingredients well with a fork. Then turn into 6 individual ramekins. Garnish the tops with the reserved orange peel and chocolate. Chill well before serving.

MAKES 6 SERVINGS.

CHOCOLATE ALMOND MARQUISE

Chocolate marquise is a classic French mousse—one of the richest— made with butter, eggs, and chocolate. It is dense and creamy. This version contains toasted almonds as an extra fillip and is served with a warm, soft custard sauce.

8 ounces semisweet chocolate, chopped into coarse pieces
4 ounces (1 stick) unsalted butter
1/2 cup toasted almonds (page 20), chopped into coarse pieces
3 large-egg whites, at room temperature
1/4 teaspoon salt
1 teaspoon vanilla extract
Sauce Anglaise (recipe follows)

1. Brush a 4-cup loaf pan with oil; invert to allow any excess to drain off.

2. Melt the chocolate with the butter in a medium-size, heavy saucepan, stirring until blended; cool. Stir in the almonds; then transfer to a mixing bowl.

3. Beat the egg whites with the salt and vanilla until stiff but not dry. Stir about one-fourth of the egg whites into the chocolate mixture; then fold in the remainder lightly but thoroughly.

4. Turn the chocolate mixture into the prepared pan, spreading it with a spatula to level it slightly; then gently shake the pan to level it completely.

5. Refrigerate the mold overnight before serving.

6. Remove the marquise from the mold by dipping a sharp knife in hot water, then cutting around the sides. Dip the bottom in a bowl of hot water; then turn out onto a serving platter or board. Cut across into 8 to 10 slices. Serve each slice on a dessert plate, with a spoonful of the warm custard sauce alongside, the remainder passed separately in a bowl.

MAKES 8 TO 10 SERVINGS.

Sauce Anglaise

4 egg yolks, at room temperature
2/3 cup sugar
5 teaspoons cornstarch
Scant 1/8 teaspoon salt
4 cups milk, heated until hot
1 1/2 teaspoons vanilla extract

1. Mix the egg yolks, sugar, cornstarch, and salt in a 3-quart heavy saucepan; do not beat.

2. Slowly pour in the hot milk, stirring constantly with a rubber spatula. Set the saucepan over direct medium heat. Stir slowly until the mixture begins to thicken; then turn the heat to low, and stir more rapidly until the sauce is thick enough to coat a spoon with a thin creamy layer.

Note: At first the mixture will foam; then, as it gradually gets hotter, the bubbles will subside, and just before it thickens, a stream of vapor will rise. The gentle heat is necessary at this point or the eggs will overcook and curdle instead of gradually turning into a smooth, velvety sauce.

3. Remove the pan from the heat, and stir the sauce rapidly to bring the temperature down slightly; then stir in the vanilla. Cover and allow the custard to cool just until warm. If preparing well in advance, set the pan in a bowl of ice water, and stir until cool. Cover and refrigerate. Reheat gently over hot water when ready to serve, just until warm, not hot.

THE CHOCOLATE MARQUISE

This recipe, similar to the previous one, is even more buttery. The mousse is set in individual molds, which, when turned out, are topped with glacéed cherries and anointed with a jigger of brandy.

8 ounces semisweet chocolate, chopped into coarse pieces
3/4 cup (1 1/2 sticks) unsalted butter, softened
1/2 cup confectioners' sugar, sifted
3 eggs, separated, at room temperature
1/2 teaspoon vanilla extract
1/8 teaspoon salt
6 to 8 candied red cherries, for garnish
Cognac

1. Melt the chocolate in the top of a double boiler set over barely simmering water. Stir to smooth; then remove from the heat, and set aside to cool slightly.

2. In a mixing bowl, with electric beaters, beat together the butter and sugar until light. Beat in the egg yolks, one at a time, beating well after each addition; then continue beating just until the mixture is creamy. Add the melted chocolate and vanilla, beating just long enough to blend in.

3. Beat the egg whites until foamy; add the salt, and continue to beat until stiff but not dry. In several additions, fold the egg whites into the chocolate mixture.

4. Spoon the mixture into 6 individual fluted 1/3-cup gelatin molds; level the tops. Refrigerate until firm, for several hours or overnight. Unmold by quickly dipping the molds into a bowl of warm water to release; then turn out onto small dessert plates. Place a candied cherry on top of each, and pour a little brandy over each.

Note: For a special presentation serve the brandy in liqueur glasses, one for each serving, so guests may use the amount desired.

MAKES 6 SERVINGS.

CHOCOLATE INNOCENCE

This is chocolate mousse in disguise, light and airy as the traditional, but with a minimum of chocolate so that the color is that of a cup of hot cocoa. And then there is rum, which gives it a delectable flavor.

6 ounces semisweet chocolate, chopped into coarse pieces
1/2 cup light or dark rum
2 cups heavy cream
1 teaspoon vanilla extract
6 large egg whites, at room temperature
1/2 teaspoon salt
1/2 teaspoon cream of tartar
2/3 cup superfine sugar
Chocolate shavings (page 12) or chocolate scrolls (page 11),
   for garnish

1. Combine the chopped chocolate and rum in the top of a double boiler. Set over lightly simmering water, and stir occasionally until the chocolate is melted and blended with the rum. Set aside to cool.

2. In a chilled bowl, with chilled beaters, whip the cream with the vanilla until it holds a soft shape. Refrigerate.

3. In a large mixer bowl beat the egg whites until foamy. Add the salt and cream of tartar, and beat until soft peaks form. Gradually beat in the sugar, and continue beating to a stiff meringue; the sugar should be completely dissolved. Taste to test.

4. Using a rubber spatula, stir about one-fourth of the meringue into the melted chocolate mixture to lighten it. Then partially fold the whipped cream into the remainder of the meringue. Add the chocolate mixture, and gently fold together until it has an even color.

5. Turn the mixture into a large serving bowl, preferably glass, mounding it lightly. Swirl the top with the spatula. Cover with plastic wrap, and chill thoroughly before serving,

several hours or overnight—even longer, because this mousse holds up extremely well.

6. When ready to serve, garnish lightly with the shaved chocolate or a few scrolls as desired. A minimum accent of dark chocolate is all that is necessary for presentation. Spoon out in mounds onto dessert plates or into dessert dishes.

MAKES 10 OR MORE SERVINGS.

COLD CHOCOLATE SOUFFLÉ WITH RUM CUSTARD

The basic chocolate soufflé mixture is baked, then intentionally allowed to fall. It is served at room temperature with a delicious rum-flavored pouring custard.

> 4 ounces semisweet chocolate
> 1/2 cup heavy cream
> 4 large eggs, separated, at room temperature
> 2 tablespoons sugar
> 3/4 teaspoon vanilla extract
> Scant 1/4 teaspoon salt
> Rum Custard (recipe follows)

1. Butter well a 1 1/2-quart soufflé dish; then sprinkle in about 1 1/2 tablespoons of granulated sugar. Rotate the dish so that the bottom and sides are lightly coated; tap out the excess. (It is important that the dish be buttered and sugared right to the rim or the soufflé will not fall evenly.) Refrigerate while preparing the soufflé mixture. Preheat the oven to 450 degrees, setting a rack one-third up from the bottom of the oven.

2. Chop the chocolate into coarse pieces, and place in a medium-size, heavy saucepan with the cream. Set over low heat, and stir to blend the ingredients once the chocolate has softened. Remove from the heat, and allow to cool slightly.

3. Using a wire whisk, beat the egg yolks with the 2 tablespoons of sugar until light. Gradually whisk in the cooled chocolate mixture and the vanilla.

4. Beat the egg whites until foamy; add the salt and beat until they are stiff but not dry. Stir about one-third of the egg whites into the chocolate mixture to lighten it; then fold in the remainder until no white traces remain.

5. Turn the soufflé mixture into the prepared dish. Place in the oven, and immediately reduce the heat to 350 degrees. Bake for 25 to 30 minutes, or until the center has risen and is firm.

6. Remove the soufflé from the oven, and place on a cooling rack. Immediately loosen the top edge with a sharp knife. As soon as it falls, invert the soufflé onto a serving platter, and cool to room temperature.

7. Cut into wedges for serving; pour a little of the custard over each. Serve the remaining sauce separately.

MAKES 6 SERVINGS.

RUM CUSTARD

1 1/2 cups milk
1/4 cup packed light brown sugar
1/8 teaspoon salt
3 egg yolks, at room temperature
1 tablespoon unsalted butter
2 tablespoons dark rum

1. Combine the milk, sugar, and salt in the top of a double boiler. Heat slowly over direct heat, stirring until bubbles appear around the edge and the sugar is dissolved.

2. Beat the egg yolks slightly in a small mixing bowl. Gradually stir part of the milk and sugar mixture into the yolks; then return to the remainder. Cook over simmering water, stirring constantly, for about 20 minutes, or until the mixture will coat a clean metal spoon. Do not allow it to boil.

3. Remove the pan from the water, and blend in the butter. Cool the mixture slightly, and stir in the rum. Cover and cool to room temperature; then chill thoroughly.

CHOCOLATE MACAROON ICEBOX TORTE

Crumbled macaroons form the base and the topping. The chocolate almond-flavored filling is molded in a ring of ladyfingers.

> 1 cup (2 sticks) unsalted butter, softened
> 1 cup confectioners' sugar, sifted
> 3 ounces unsweetened chocolate
> 1 ounce semisweet chocolate
> 4 large eggs, at room temperature
> 1 teaspoon vanilla extract
> 1/2 teaspoon almond extract
> 12 double 3-inch ladyfingers
> 12 almond macaroons
> 1/2 cup heavy cream, for garnish

1. In the large bowl of an electric mixer cream the butter with the sugar. Set aside.

2. Chop the chocolates into coarse pieces, and melt in a small, heavy saucepan over very low heat. Cool slightly; then beat into the butter mixture.

3. Add the eggs, one at a time, beating for 1 minute after each addition, then for 5 minutes on medium speed after the last egg has been added. Beat in the vanilla and almond extracts.

4. Split the ladyfingers, and arrange vertically around the sides of an 8-inch springform pan, sugar side next to the metal. (You will need 20; they will stand better if not separated.) Crumble the remaining ladyfingers, and sprinkle over the bottom of the torte pan.

5. Crumble 3 of the almond macaroons into fairly fine crumbs and set aside for garnish. Crumble the remainder into coarse crumbs, and sprinkle over the crumbled ladyfingers. Spoon the chocolate mixture into the pan, and spread the top to level it. Refrigerate for at least 6 hours, or until firm, or several days, if desired.

6. When ready to serve or several hours in advance, whip the cream until stiff. Spread over the top of the filling, and garnish with the reserved macaroon crumbs.

7. To serve, remove the rim from the springform pan, and cut the chilled torte into wedges.

MAKES 10 SERVINGS.

TURINOIS

A specialty dessert which originated in the northern part of Italy. Its unique flavor is attributed to the use of puréed chestnuts, which, combined with butter, chocolate, and vanilla, make it so rich that small servings suffice.

> *1 15 1/2-ounce can chestnut purée**
> *1/2 cup (1 stick) unsalted butter, softened*
> *1/2 cup sugar*
> *1/8 teaspoon salt*
> *4 ounces semisweet chocolate, grated (page 9)*
> *1 1/2 teaspoons vanilla extract*
> *Sweetened Whipped Cream (recipe follows)*

1. Brush a 4- to 5-cup loaf pan lightly with oil; invert to drain off any excess.
2. Place the chestnut purée in a heavy saucepan. Heat over low heat, breaking up the purée and mashing it with a fork. Add the butter, in chunks, and blend in. Then add the sugar, salt, and grated chocolate. Continue heating and stirring until the ingredients are well blended and smooth. Remove from the heat, and stir in the vanilla.

Note: If the mixture is not creamy-smooth, process briefly in a food processor.

3. Turn the mixture into the pan, and smooth the top. Refrigerate until firm, preferably overnight. However, it keeps well, chilled, for at least a week.
4. To remove the Turinois from the mold, dip a sharp knife in hot water; then cut around the sides to release. Briefly dip the bottom of the mold in a bowl of hot water to release it; invert onto a flat surface. Cut into thick slices for serving; place

---

*Chestnut purée can be bought in vacuum-sealed cans in food specialty shops and gourmet sections in some department stores.

each on a dessert plate, with a spoonful of whipped cream alongside. Serve very cold.

MAKES 8 TO 10 SERVINGS.

SWEETENED WHIPPED CREAM

1 1/2 cups heavy cream
3 tablespoons confectioners' sugar
1 1/4 teaspoons vanilla extract

Pour the cream into a chilled mixing bowl. Press the sugar through a wire sieve into the cream. Add the vanilla. Beat with chilled beaters until the cream mounds softly, not until stiff. Serve immediately.

Note: The cream may be whipped several hours in advance and refrigerated. If it has begun to separate, beat it briefly with a wire whisk before using.

FRENCH CHOCOLATE FONDANT

An unusual dessert with a surprising foundation: puréed potatoes, an ingredient sometimes used by candymakers for the fondant centers of coated chocolates. The flavor and texture are similar to those of boiled chestnuts, which are prized by many French and Italian cooks.

1/2 pound (about 2 medium) baking potatoes
6 tablespoons (3/4 stick) unsalted butter, softened
3/4 cup superfine sugar
*1/2 teaspoon instant espresso powder, dissolved in 2
    teaspoons hot water*
1 teaspoon vanilla extract
2 egg yolks
2 1/2 ounces unsweetened chocolate, melted and cooled
1/2 cup heavy cream, whipped, for garnish

1. Brush a 3- to 4-cup loaf pan lightly with oil; invert to drain off any excess.

2. Peel and quarter the potatoes. Drop into boiling salted water to cover, and boil for about 20 minutes, or until tender. Drain and immediately put through a potato ricer or food mill into a bowl. Let stand while preparing the remaining ingredients.

3. In a large mixing bowl, with electric beaters, cream the butter, gradually adding first the sugar, then the dissolved coffee and vanilla. Add the egg yolks, and beat at medium-high speed for about 5 minutes, or until the mixture is very smooth and creamy. Blend in first the melted chocolate, then the riced potatoes, and continue beating just until all the ingredients are well blended.

4. Turn the fondant into the prepared loaf pan; shake the pan slightly to level it. (The mixture will only partially fill the pan but should be about 1 1/4 to 1 1/2 inches deep.) Refrigerate for at least several hours until firm, preferably overnight.

5. When ready to serve, the fondant should have pulled

slightly away from the sides of the pan. Dip the bottom of the pan into warm water to loosen; then turn out onto a small serving platter or wooden board. Run the tines of a fork lengthwise across the top, then along the sides—a simple decoration to keep the fondant from looking plain.

6. Cut into thick slices, and serve each slice with a dollop of unsweetened whipped cream, either dropped from a spoon or made into a rosette by being put through a pastry tube.

MAKES 6 TO 8 SERVINGS.

MARZIPAN TORTE

A two-layer dessert molded in a loaf pan. The ground almond confection, marzipan, serves as a base for bittersweet chocolate buttercream. It is exquisitely rich, so small servings will do.

CHOCOLATE BUTTERCREAM

6 ounces semisweet chocolate, chopped into coarse pieces
3 tablespoons light or dark rum
3/4 cup (1 1/2 sticks) unsalted butter, softened
6 tablespoons superfine sugar
3 eggs, separated, at room temperature

MARZIPAN

1 1/4 cups fine-chopped blanched almonds (page 20)
1 cup confectioners' sugar, sifted
1 egg yolk, at room temperature
1 tablespoon unsalted butter, melted
2 teaspoons grated lemon rind
1 tablespoon light or dark rum
1/4 cup sliced toasted almonds (page 20), for garnish

1. Brush a 6-cup loaf pan lightly with oil; invert to drain off any excess.
2. *For the buttercream:* Melt the chocolate with the 3 tablespoons rum in the top of a double boiler set over hot water. Set aside to cool slightly.

In a small mixing bowl cream the 3/4 cup butter and 4 tablespoons of the superfine sugar until light and fluffy. Beat in the egg yolks one at a time. Blend in the melted chocolate mixture.

In a separate bowl beat the egg whites until fluffy. Gradually beat in the remaining 2 tablespoons superfine sugar, and continue beating until the mixture is stiff and the sugar is dissolved. Stir a little of the meringue into the chocolate mixture to lighten it; then fold in the remainder, gently but thoroughly. Turn into the prepared loaf pan, and spread evenly with a spatula, or shake to form a thick, level layer. Refrigerate or freeze until firm.

3. *For the marzipan:* Mix together the ground almonds and confectioners' sugar in a small mixing bowl, using a fork. Add the egg yolk, melted butter, grated lemon rind, and 1 tablespoon rum. Stir with the fork until the mixture is well blended and holds together. Spoon onto the top of the chilled chocolate mixture. Smooth it over, and press evenly with a spatula (the mixture will be turned out, so it should be as level as possible). Refrigerate overnight.

4. To serve, remove the torte from the mold by dipping a sharp knife in hot water, then cutting around the sides. Dip the bottom in a bowl of hot water; then turn out onto a serving platter or board. Press the sliced almonds onto the sides of the chocolate layer. Cut across into thin slices. Serve immediately so that the chocolate layer remains firm.

MAKES 10 OR MORE SERVINGS.

DACQUOISE AU CHOCOLAT

Dacquoise is among the favorite desserts in fine restaurants. It is a layered meringue dessert made with nuts and rich buttercream. In this version, toasted hazelnuts are used in the meringues and the buttercream is made with chocolate. Rum-flavored whipped cream is used for part of the filling.

MERINGUE LAYERS

1 1/2 cups plus 8 to 10 hazelnuts, for garnish
3/4 cup granulated sugar
1 tablespoon cornstarch
6 egg whites (7/8 cup), at room temperature
1/4 teaspoon cream of tartar

CHOCOLATE BUTTERCREAM

3 ounces semisweet chocolate, chopped into coarse pieces
1/2 cup granulated sugar
1/4 cup water
3 egg yolks, at room temperature
8 ounces (2 sticks) unsalted butter, at cool room temperature

ASSEMBLY AND GARNISH

1 cup heavy cream
1 tablespoon confectioners' sugar
2 tablespoons light rum
Confectioners' sugar and unsweetened cocoa powder, for
   garnish

1. Preheat the oven to 350 degrees, setting two racks, one just above and one just below the center. Grease and flour two cookie sheets, tapping off the excess flour. Mark a 10-inch circle on each sheet, using a dinner plate as a guide.

2. *For the meringue:* Place the hazelnuts in a shallow baking pan. Bake on the lower rack for 10 minutes, shaking occasionally to toast evenly. Cool slightly; then put in a cloth towel, and rub lightly to remove most of the skins. Reserve the hazelnuts required for garnish; then grate the remainder in a food processor until fine (or grind one-fourth at a time in an electric blender). Mix together with the 3/4 cup granulated sugar and cornstarch; set aside.

Beat the egg whites with the cream of tartar until stiff (test by turning the bowl upside down; they will adhere if properly beaten). With a rubber spatula, gently fold in the nut mixture. Spoon half the meringue onto each cookie sheet, spreading it evenly to fill the marked circles completely.

Bake at 350 degrees for 20 to 25 minutes, or until the meringues are browned and the tops feel dry. Let the meringues set for a few minutes; then loosen with a spatula; slide them off the sheets to wire racks to cool. (They will be pliable at first but firm upon cooling.) Let stand for at least 1 hour.

3. *For the buttercream:* Melt the chocolate in a small, heavy saucepan set over very low heat; set aside to cool.

Combine the 1/2 cup granulated sugar and water in a small saucepan. Bring to a boil, stirring, over medium heat. Then boil without stirring until the syrup reaches a temperature of 230 to 234 degrees on a candy thermometer, or until it spins a thread when dropped from a fork; remove from the heat.

Place the egg yolks in the small bowl of an electric mixer. Beat at medium speed, while slowly pouring in the hot syrup. Continue beating for 6 to 8 minutes, or until the eggs are as thick as a light mayonnaise and are pale yellow.

Beat in 1 stick of the butter, a tablespoon at a time. Then beat in the cooled melted chocolate. Add the remaining butter, again by tablespoonfuls, and continue beating just long enough so that the butter is incorporated and the mixture is smooth. Set aside at room temperature until ready to use.

Note: It is important that the butter be at a cool room temperature, not meltingly soft. (If it is too cold, however, the buttercream may curdle.)

4. *For assembly and garnish:* Whip the cream with the 1 tablespoon confectioners' sugar and rum until stiff but not buttery. Set aside.

Place one meringue layer, flat side down, on a large round serving plate. Spread about half the buttercream around the perimeter, about 1 1/2 inches. Spoon, then spread the whipped cream to fill the center. Place the second layer, rounded side up, on top. Spread the remaining buttercream smoothly over the top.

Dust the top of the assembled torte heavily with a coating of confectioners' sugar put through a wire sieve. Garnish the top of this with a thin dusting of the cocoa, using just enough to coat it unevenly, so that the white coating dominates. Decorate the torte with the reserved hazelnuts, spaced so that there will be one for each serving.

5. Refrigerate the torte for at least 1 hour or several hours, if desired, and serve cold. Cut into wedges for serving, using a serrated knife.

Note: The torte may be refrigerated overnight, but the meringues will lose their slightly crisp quality—perfectly acceptable but second best.

MAKES 8 TO 10 SERVINGS.

MILK CHOCOLATE BAVARIAN

A classic Bavarian cream: rich custard mixed with gelatin, whipped cream, and chocolate. Milk bar chocolate is used here instead of the usual dark chocolate. The molded dessert, cut into wedges, is served with a contrasting bittersweet chocolate sauce.

> 1 envelope unflavored gelatin
> 1/4 cup cold water
> 5 egg yolks, at room temperature
> 1/2 cup sugar
> 1 cup milk
> 8 ounces milk chocolate, chopped into coarse pieces
> 1 3/4 cups heavy cream
> Bittersweet Chocolate Sauce (recipe follows)

1. Brush a 1 1/2-quart soufflé dish lightly with oil. Invert to drain off any excess.

2. Sprinkle the gelatin over the cold water; set aside to soften.

3. In a medium-size mixer bowl beat the egg yolks with the sugar on high speed until thick and pale. The batter should form a ribbon on the surface when the beaters are raised.

4. Heat the milk in a small saucepan until bubbles appear around the edge. With the mixer on low, gradually beat the milk into the egg yolk mixture. Transfer to a 1 1/2-quart heavy saucepan. Cook, stirring, over low heat until the mixture thickens and will coat a spoon. Do not allow it to boil, or the custard will curdle. Remove from the heat.

5. Add the softened gelatin, and stir until melted. Add the chocolate, and whisk until the chocolate is melted and the custard is smooth. Transfer to a large mixing bowl, and refrigerate until slightly thickened but still viscous, similar to the consistency of unbeaten egg whites. (If overchilled, it will not blend smoothly with the whipped cream.)

6. Whip the heavy cream until it mounds slightly. Fold into the gelatin mixture. Pour into the soufflé dish, and shake slightly to level. Cover and refrigerate for at least 6 hours or until firm, or for several days, if preferred.

7. Unmold the Bavarian when ready to serve or a few hours in advance; it holds up well when unmolded (cover it with an inverted bowl, and refrigerate). To unmold, cut around the sides with a sharp knife; then rub the bottom and sides with a hot damp towel just long enough to loosen the Bavarian. Invert the dish onto a lightly oiled plate to turn out.

8. To serve, cut the Bavarian into eight wedges, and place, cut sides down, on individual serving plates. Pour about 1/4 cup of the chocolate sauce over each; serve immediately.

MAKES 8 SERVINGS.

BITTERSWEET CHOCOLATE SAUCE

1/2 cup sugar
1 cup water
6 ounces semisweet chocolate, chopped into coarse pieces
2 ounces unsweetened chocolate, chopped into coarse pieces
4 tablespoons (1/2 stick) unsalted butter, cut into chunks
1 tablespoon cognac or other brandy

1. Combine the sugar and water in a 1 1/2-quart saucepan. Cook over high heat, stirring, until the sugar dissolves and heavy bubbles appear around the edge. Cover and reduce the heat to low; simmer for 5 minutes. Uncover and remove from the heat; cool to lukewarm.

2. Melt the chocolates with the butter in a small, heavy saucepan set over very low heat. Stir occasionally until the chocolate is melted and the mixture is smooth; remove from the heat.

3. Gradually stir the lukewarm syrup into the chocolate mixture. When it is blended, stir in the cognac. Cover the pan, and allow it to cool at room temperature until lukewarm before using. It should be slightly thickened but still pourable. (If it should thicken too much, reheat briefly to bring to the proper consistency.)

Note: The sauce keeps well at room temperature for at least 2 days. Reheat as suggested. Do not refrigerate because it will harden.

CHOCOLATE CHRISTMAS PUDDING

A ring of chocolate pudding filled with raisins, dates, and walnuts.

> 1 envelope unflavored gelatin
> 1/2 cup cold water
> 1 ounce unsweetened chocolate, chopped into coarse pieces
> 1 cup milk
> 1/2 cup sugar
> 1/8 teaspoon salt
> 3/4 cup raisins
> 1/3 cup coarse-cut dates
> 1/2 teaspoon vanilla extract
> 1/4 cup chopped walnuts
> 2 large-egg whites, at room temperature
> Sweetened Whipped Cream (recipe follows)
> A sprig of holly, for optional garnish

1. Lightly oil a 4-cup ring mold; invert so that the excess oil drains off.

2. Sprinkle the gelatin over the cold water; set aside to soften.

3. Combine the chocolate and milk in a 1 1/2-quart heavy saucepan. Set over moderate heat; cook, stirring occasionally, until the chocolate has melted and the mixture comes just to a boil, thickens slightly, and is smooth. Remove from the heat, and add the softened gelatin, 1/4 cup of the sugar, and the salt. Stir until all have dissolved. Then stir in the raisins and dates.

4. Place the pan of chocolate mixture in a bowl partly filled with ice and cold water. Stir frequently until the mixture is cold and has slightly thickened. Then stir in the vanilla and chopped walnuts.

5. While the chocolate mixture is cooling, beat the egg whites until they mound in soft peaks. Gradually add the remaining 1/4 cup sugar, a tablespoon at a time; then continue

beating until a stiff meringue forms and the sugar has dissolved. Fold into the gelatin mixture until it is evenly colored.

6. Spoon the mixture into the ring mold, making certain that the dried fruits and nuts are evenly distributed. Refrigerate for several hours until set, overnight if preferred.

7. To serve the mold, shake to loosen; then turn out onto a serving plate. If necessary, rub the outside of the mold with a warm damp towel.

8. Prepare the whipped cream as directed, and spoon into a bowl small enough to fit into the center of the ring. (See recipe for advance preparation.) Garnish the top with the sprig of holly.

MAKES 8 SERVINGS.

SWEETENED WHIPPED CREAM

1 cup heavy cream
2 tablespoons confectioners' sugar
1/2 teaspoon vanilla extract

In a chilled small bowl, with chilled beaters, whip the cream, sugar, and vanilla only until the cream holds a soft shape. Serve immediately, or refrigerate in the bowl until ready to serve, several hours in advance, if desired. (If it separates, beat with a wire whisk just long enough to smooth and restore the soft thickness.)

GÂTEAU MOULE AU CHOCOLAT

Almost like a steamed pudding but more moist and dense, this French "ring of chocolate" is served cold and may be made a day or two in advance. Its accompaniment is a warm buttery rum sauce, which may make you wonder which you like the best.

2 ounces unsweetened chocolate, chopped into coarse pieces
6 tablespoons (3/4 stick) unsalted butter
2/3 cup sifted all-purpose flour
3/4 cup milk
1/4 cup plus 2 tablespoons sugar
1 teaspoon vanilla extract
4 large eggs, separated, at room temperature
1/4 teaspoon salt
Butter Rum Sauce (recipe follows)

1. Lightly grease a 5-cup ring mold, dust with sugar, and tap out the excess. Preheat the oven to 350 degrees, with a rack set in the center.

2. Melt the chocolate with the butter in a 1 1/2-quart heavy saucepan set over low heat. Remove from the heat, and blend in the flour. Heat the milk in a separate saucepan until bubbles appear around the edge. Gradually stir into the chocolate mixture.

3. Return the pan to low heat, and cook briefly, stirring, until the mixture begins to pull away from the sides of the pan. Remove from the heat, and stir in the 1/4 cup sugar and vanilla. Add the egg yolks, one at a time, and beat until the mixture is creamy. Transfer to a large mixing bowl.

4. Beat the egg whites with the salt until soft peaks form. Gradually add the remaining 2 tablespoons sugar, and beat until stiff. In three or four additions, stir in about one-third of the meringue to lighten the chocolate mixture (it is very stiff); then fold in the remainder. Spoon into the ring mold; spread it

evenly; then shake it slightly to settle; it must be level to bake evenly.

5. Set the ring mold into a larger pan, and add hot water to a depth of about 2 inches. Bake for 45 to 50 minutes until the gâteau is firm and a wooden pick comes out clean. Remove from the water, and let it stand for a few minutes; then unmold onto a serving plate, and let stand until completely cooled. (The dessert may be made a day or two in advance.)

6. When ready to serve, prepare the rum sauce; turn it into a small bowl, and place it in the center of the chocolate ring. Cut into thick slices, and spoon about 2 tablespoons of the warm sauce over each serving.

MAKES 6 TO 8 SERVINGS.

BUTTER RUM SAUCE

1/2 cup sugar
4 teaspoons cornstarch
1/4 teaspoon salt
3/4 cup plus 2 tablespoons water
2 tablespoons butter
2 tablespoons heavy cream
2 tablespoons light rum
1 teaspoon vanilla extract

Combine the sugar, cornstarch, and salt in a small, heavy saucepan. Stir in the water. Cook, stirring, over medium heat for about 5 minutes, or until the sauce thickens and is clear. Remove from the heat, and stir in the butter. When the butter is melted, stir in the cream, rum, and vanilla extract. Serve warm.

Note: The sauce may be reheated. Do not boil, or it will thin.

CASSIS WHITE CHOCOLATE CHEESECAKE

An exceptionally creamy, rich, and sweet cheesecake. The white chocolate flavor is there but just barely noticeable. The consistency of the filling is such that it will melt in your mouth.

VANILLA CRUMB CRUST

2 cups vanilla wafer crumbs
1/4 cup sugar
1/2 cup (1 stick) unsalted butter, melted

WHITE CHOCOLATE FILLING

2 pounds cream cheese, at room temperature
1 cup sugar
4 ounces (3/4 cup) grated white chocolate (page 9)
3 tablespoons crème de cassis, a currant liqueur
4 large eggs, at room temperature

SOUR CREAM TOPPING

2 cups (1 pint) dairy sour cream
1/4 cup sugar
1 teaspoon vanilla extract

1. *For the crust:* Combine the crumbs and sugar in a mixing bowl. Add the melted butter, mixing with a fork to distribute well. Press onto the bottom and halfway up the sides of

an ungreased 9-inch springform pan (the top edge need not be even). Set aside.

2. *For the filling:* Preheat the oven to 350 degrees, setting a rack one-third up from the bottom.

In the large bowl of an electric mixer cream the softened cream cheese until it is very smooth. Gradually beat in the 1 cup sugar, then the grated white chocolate and cassis, beating just until well blended. Beat in the eggs, one at a time, and continue beating until smooth.

3. Pour the filling into the crust. Tap the pan lightly on the counter two or three times to eliminate any large air bubbles. Bake for 40 to 45 minutes. (The edges may have a few cracks, but the center of the filling will not appear set.) Remove and place the pan on a rack, away from drafts, to cool for 10 minutes. Do not turn off the oven.

4. *For the topping:* Combine the sour cream, the 1/4 cup sugar, and vanilla in a small mixing bowl. Stir with a spoon until blended. Pour over the top of the slightly cooled filling, and spread evenly to the edges.

5. Return the cheesecake to the 350-degree oven, and bake for 10 minutes longer. The topping will quiver but should appear set.

6. Return the baked cheesecake to the rack, and allow it to cool completely. Cover the pan loosely with foil; refrigerate for at least 12 hours before serving.

7. To serve, carefully remove the sides of the pan, cut the cake into wedges, and serve immediately. The cheesecake is creamy-soft even in its chilled state.

MAKES 12 OR MORE SERVINGS.

CHOCOLATE IN CHOCOLATE CHEESECAKE

This intensely flavored cheesecake requires a topping of softly whipped cream for contrast of texture and to subdue the richness. It is an ideal dessert for a large buffet since it serves sixteen and should be made several days in advance.

CHOCOLATE CRUMB CRUST

2 cups chocolate wafer crumbs
1/2 teaspoon ground cinnamon
1/2 cup (1 stick) unsalted butter, melted

CHOCOLATE CHEESE FILLING

6 ounces unsweetened chocolate
6 ounces semisweet chocolate
2 pounds cream cheese, at room temperature
2 teaspoons vanilla extract
1/4 teaspoon salt
2 cups granulated sugar
1 tablespoon unsweetened cocoa powder
4 large eggs, at room temperature
2 cups (1 pint) dairy sour cream
*1 tablespoon confectioners' sugar, mixed with 1 tablespoon
    unsweetened cocoa powder, for garnish*
Soft Whipped Cream (recipe follows), for garnish

1. *For the crust:* Grease only the sides of a 10 × 3-inch springform pan. Be certain to grease the sides well to the rim, or the batter may not rise evenly. The pan must be the proper size because the filling rises to the top during baking.

Combine the crumbs and cinnamon well in a mixing bowl. Add the melted butter, mixing to distribute evenly. Press the mixture onto the bottom and about halfway up the sides of the springform pan. The mixture should be a little thicker where the bottom and sides meet. Refrigerate to firm while preparing the filling.

2. *For the filling:* First preheat the oven to 350 degrees, setting a rack one-third up from the bottom.

Chop the two kinds of chocolate into coarse pieces. Place in the top of a double boiler. Set the pan over hot water, and place over low heat. Cover until partially melted; then uncover and stir until completely melted and smooth. Remove the pan from the hot water, and set aside to cool slightly.

In the large bowl of an electric mixer cream the softened cream cheese until it is very smooth. Add the vanilla and salt. Gradually beat in 1 1/2 cups of the granulated sugar, beating until blended. Combine the cocoa with the remaining 1/2 cup granulated sugar, and beat in. Blend in the chocolate. Then beat in the eggs, one at a time. Add the sour cream, and beat again just until smooth.

3. Pour the filling into the chilled crust, leveling the top. Bake for 1 hour and 10 minutes. The edges should seem firm, but the center soft and quivery. Turn off the oven, and pull the oven door slightly ajar. Allow the cheesecake to cool for 10 minutes; then remove to a cooling rack.

Note: A thin crust will form and may be slightly cracked at the edges; and the center will sink slightly as the cheesecake cools. This is to be expected.

4. Allow the cheesecake to stand until tepid. Then cover the top of the pan with foil, and refrigerate for at least 12 hours before serving.

Note: This cheesecake actually tastes better if it is made several days in advance. Any leftovers may be returned to the refrigerator for several more days; or the cheesecake, wrapped airtight, may be frozen for at least a month (thaw overnight in the refrigerator before removing the covering and serving).

5. To serve, remove the sides of the springform pan. Ga nish the top with the mixture of confectioners' sugar and cocoa

pressed through a wire sieve. Cut into wedges, and serve cold, with the whipped cream served separately. The cream is only lightly whipped and serves more as a sauce than a stiff garnish and should be used lavishly.

MAKES 16 OR MORE SERVINGS.

SOFT WHIPPED CREAM

3 cups heavy cream
6 tablespoons confectioners' sugar
1 1/2 teaspoons vanilla extract

Whip the cream with the sugar and vanilla just until very soft peaks form. Serve immediately.

Note: The cream may be whipped several hours in advance, but then should be whipped until slightly firmer. Refrigerate; then whisk again before using just long enough to incorporate any liquid from the bottom of the bowl.

ALMOND MARBLE CHEESECAKE

Almonds in the chocolate crust and amaretto liqueur in the cheese fill-
ing, made attractive with swirls of melted chocolate.

CHOCOLATE CRUMB CRUST

3/4 cup chocolate wafer crumbs
1/2 cup fine-chopped blanched almonds (page 20)
3 tablespoons sugar
3 tablespoons unsalted butter, melted

MARBLE CHEESE FILLING

1 1/2 pounds cream cheese, at room temperature
3/4 cup sugar
3 tablespoons all-purpose flour, sifted
3 tablespoons amaretto or other almond-flavored liqueur
3 eggs, at room temperature
1 ounce unsweetened chocolate, melted

1. *For the crust:* First preheat the oven to 350 degrees, setting a rack one-third up from the bottom.

Combine the wafer crumbs, chopped almonds, the 3 tablespoons sugar, and melted butter in a bowl, mixing with a fork
until well blended. Press onto only the bottom of a 10-inch
springform pan. Bake for 10 minutes. Remove from the oven,
and cool on a rack. Butter halfway up, then attach the sides of
the pan. Increase the oven heat to 450 degrees.

2. *For the filling:* In the large bowl of an electric mixer

cream the softened cream cheese until it is smooth. Add the 3/4 cup sugar, flour, and amaretto; beat just until well blended. Blend in the eggs, one at a time.

Remove 1 cup of the batter to a small mixing bowl, and blend in the melted chocolate. Pour the plain batter over the crust. Then spoon the chocolate mixture on in four separate mounds. Cut through the batter with a knife, swirling it several times for a marbled effect.

3. Bake the cheesecake at 450 degrees for 10 minutes. Then reduce the temperature to 250 degrees (without opening the oven door), and continue baking for 25 to 30 minutes, or just until the filling is set. If overbaked, the cheesecake will crack.

4. Remove the pan from the oven, and cool on a rack, away from drafts, to room temperature. Refrigerate until well chilled, overnight if preferred.

Note: Unlike other cheesecakes, this one tends to dry within a day or two.

5. When ready to serve, carefully loosen the sides of the pan, and cut the cake into wedges. The cheesecake is served without garnish because the marbled filling alone provides an attractive appearance.

MAKES 10 OR MORE SERVINGS.

VI

FROZEN DESSERTS

GLACÉ AU CHOCOLAT
AMARETTO ALMOND FREEZE
FROZEN CHOCOLATE SABAYON
MILE-HIGH BLACK BOTTOM ALASKA
MERINGUES GLACÉES
BROWNIE SUNDAES
ICE CREAM SANDWICHES
SYDNEY'S MARK III
GRAND MARNIER CHOCOLATE MOUSSE TORTE
WHITE CHOCOLATE MOUSSE TART
FROZEN CHOCOLATE CHEESE PIE
BLACK BOTTOM LEMON CURD PIE
PEANUT BUTTER CRUNCH PIE

GLACÉ AU CHOCOLAT

This is a French ice cream that is easy to make. It needs no churning or second whippings once it is put in the freezer. The result is very smooth and rich. It may be served plain or with chocolate dipped strawberries as garnish. The ultimate in frozen confection.

12 ounces semisweet chocolate, chopped into coarse pieces
4 ounces unsweetened chocolate, chopped into coarse pieces
1/4 cup water
1 tablespoon vanilla extract
4 cups heavy cream
1 1/2 cups sugar
10 to 12 large Chocolate Dipped Strawberries (page 14)

1. Combine the chocolates with the water in the top of a double boiler. Set over barely simmering water, and stir occasionally until the chocolate is melted and the mixture is smooth. Remove from the heat, and stir in the vanilla. Cool while whipping the cream.

2. In a chilled large mixing bowl, with electric beaters, beat the cream until it begins to thicken. Gradually beat in the sugar, and continue beating until the cream holds a soft shape.

3. With a rubber spatula, stir a large spoonful of the whipped cream into the cooled chocolate. Then stir in two or three more spoonfuls, adding just enough so that the chocolate is smooth and mounds lightly, like the whipped cream. Pour this mixture into the remaining whipped cream; fold in until it has an even color.

4. Pour the mixture into a metal container (a mixing bowl is perfect) with at least a 2-quart capacity. Smooth the top, and cover the container tightly with foil. Freeze for several hours until firm. It keeps well for several days.

5. To serve, scoop the frozen mixture into wine goblets, and top each serving with a chocolate-coated strawberry.

MAKES 2 QUARTS OR 10 TO 12 SERVINGS.

AMARETTO ALMOND FREEZE

An easy dessert, simple to make but special.

1 quart French vanilla ice cream
18 chocolate cookie wafers*
1/2 cup heavy cream
1 tablespoon confectioners' sugar
1/4 teaspoon vanilla extract
2 teaspoons unsalted butter
6 tablespoons blanched, slivered almonds
Salt
About 6 tablespoons amaretto, an almond-flavored liqueur

1. Place the ice cream in the refrigerator just long enough to soften slightly. Crumble the chocolate wafers by hand (they should be in coarse pieces, about 1 inch in size); set aside.

2. Whip the cream with the sugar and vanilla in a chilled small bowl until it holds a firm shape.

3. In a chilled large bowl of an electric mixer whip the ice cream until smooth but not melted. Quickly, on the lowest speed, mix in the whipped cream. By hand fold in the wafer pieces. Place the bowl in the freezer, and freeze for a few hours, or until firm.

4. Melt the butter in a small skillet set over low heat. Add the almonds; stir constantly until the nuts are lightly golden. Remove from the heat, and stir to prevent further browning. Salt lightly, and set aside to cool.

5. To serve, scoop the ice cream mixture into large wine goblets or individual bowls. Pour about 1 tablespoon of the amaretto over each serving, and top with the toasted almonds.

MAKES 6 SERVINGS.

*Nabisco's famous chocolate wafers are required; they may be found in most supermarkets.

FROZEN CHOCOLATE SABAYON

An unusual frozen "ice cream" fully flavored with Italian Marsala and only a hint of chocolate. The dessert contains candied cherries, candied pineapple, and toasted almonds.

> *2 large-egg yolks, at room temperature*
> *1 tablespoon sugar*
> *1 1/2 teaspoons cold water*
> *1/4 cup Marsala or port wine*
> *1 ounce semisweet chocolate, grated (page 9)*
> *1/3 cup diced candied pineapple*
> *1/3 cup diced candied cherries*
> *1/2 cup slivered, toasted almonds (page 20)*
> *1 cup heavy cream*
> *Chocolate shavings (page 12), for garnish*

1. Lightly oil an 8-inch springform pan; invert to drain off any excess oil.

2. Place the egg yolks, sugar, and cold water in a large heatproof mixing bowl. Stir together, using a wire whisk; then gradually stir in the wine. Set the bowl over a saucepan of barely simmering water. Beat with the whisk for about 2 to 3 minutes, or until the mixture is thick and creamy.

3. Remove the bowl from the saucepan, add the grated chocolate, and stir until melted. Set the bowl in a separate bowl partially filled with ice and water; stir occasionally until cool.

4. Stir the diced pineapple, cherries, and almonds into the sabayon mixture. Whip the cream until stiff; fold it in.

5. Pour the mixture into the prepared pan; garnish the top with the shaved chocolate; then freeze for at least 8 hours, or until firm, or overnight, if desired.

6. When ready to serve, run a sharp knife around the edges of the sabayon to loosen it; then remove the sides from the springform pan. Cut into wedges, and place on dessert plates. Allow to stand a few minutes before serving so that the sabayon is meltingly soft.

MAKES 6 SERVINGS.

MILE-HIGH BLACK BOTTOM ALASKA

A departure from the usual baked Alaska. Here the ice cream is mounded high in a chocolate crumb crust, covered with meringue, baked, and served with a bittersweet chocolate sauce.

PECAN CHOCOLATE CRUMB CRUST

2 cups chocolate wafer crumbs
1 cup pecans, chopped into fine pieces
1/2 cup (1 stick) unsalted butter, melted

ICE CREAM FILLING

3 pints chocolate chip vanilla ice cream

MERINGUE TOPPING

6 egg whites (7/8 cup), at room temperature
1/2 teaspoon cream of tartar
1 cup sugar
Bittersweet Chocolate Sauce (recipe follows)

1. *For the crust:* Combine the wafer crumbs and chopped pecans in a mixing bowl. Add the melted butter, and mix with a fork until crumbly. Turn into a 9-inch springform pan (sides attached), and press the mixture firmly onto only the bottom with the back of a spoon. Refrigerate or freeze until firm.

2. *For the filling:* Refrigerate the ice cream in the cartons just until soft enough to spoon out. Remove the sides from the springform pan; then cover the crust with the ice cream, mounding it high in the center and leaving a 3/4-inch edge. Smooth the ice cream with a wet spatula to create a dome. Cover with plastic wrap, and freeze for at least a few hours, or until solidly frozen, or for several days, if desired, before completing the dessert.

3. *For the meringue:* Preheat the oven to 500 degrees, setting a rack in the center. In the large bowl of an electric mixer beat the egg whites with the cream of tartar until nearly stiff. Gradually beat in the sugar, a few tablespoons at a time. Then continue beating until you have a meringue that is stiff and glossy.

4. Spread the meringue over the ice cream and the crust to cover completely, swirling it decoratively.

5. Place the dessert on a baking sheet, and bake for 3 to 5 minutes, or just until the meringue is delicately browned. Serve immediately. Or if preferred, return to the freezer for 1 or 2 hours before serving.

6. To serve, cut into wedges, using a firm sharp knife. If the crust does not cut through easily, let it stand briefly. Top each portion with a spoonful or two of the chocolate sauce. Pass the remainder in a sauceboat.

MAKES 12 TO 16 SERVINGS.

BITTERSWEET CHOCOLATE SAUCE

1/2 cup sugar
1 cup water
4 ounces semisweet chocolate, chopped into coarse pieces
4 ounces unsweetened chocolate, chopped into coarse pieces
1/4 cup (1/2 stick) unsalted butter, cut into chunks
2 teaspoons vanilla extract

1. Combine the sugar and water in a 1 1/2-quart sauce-pan. Set over high heat, and stir until the sugar has dissolved and heavy bubbles appear around the edge. Cover the pan, and reduce the heat to low; simmer for 5 minutes. Uncover and re-move from the heat; cool to lukewarm.

2. Melt the chocolates with the butter in a small, heavy saucepan set over very low heat. Stir occasionally until the choc-olate is melted and the mixture is smooth; remove from the heat.

3. Gradually stir the lukewarm syrup into the chocolate mixture. When it is blended, stir in the vanilla. Cover the pan, and allow the mixture to cool at room temperature until luke-warm before it is used. It should be slightly thickened but still pourable. (If it should thicken too much, reheat briefly to bring to the proper consistency.)

Note: The sauce keeps well at room temperature for at least 2 days. Reheat as suggested. Do not refrigerate because it will harden.

MERINGUES GLACÉES

Elegant, individual desserts made with snowy-white meringues, vanilla ice cream, and bittersweet chocolate sauce. The meringues are sandwiched together with a scoop of ice cream and set in a pool of the chocolate sauce. Meringues and sauce keep well and may be prepared in advance.

> 12 *Crisp Meringues (recipe follows)*
> *Cognac Chocolate Sauce (recipe follows)*
> 6 *scoops French vanilla ice cream*

1. Prepare the meringue shells and chocolate sauce in advance, as directed. Use two meringue shells for each serving, one scoop of ice cream, and a pool of the chocolate sauce poured onto each of six dessert plates.

2. To assemble, spoon about 1/4 cup of the chocolate sauce onto each plate, reserving just enough to drizzle over the tops as a token garnish. Place a rounded scoop of the ice cream in the center. Quickly place a meringue shell on each side, pressing slightly to sandwich together. Spoon the remaining sauce over the tops, just enough to give the glacées a finishing touch.

Note: In order to make perfect round scoops of the ice cream, you will need to purchase one quart.

MAKES 6 SERVINGS.

CRISP MERINGUES

> 3 *extra-large-egg whites*
> 3/4 *cup superfine sugar*
> 3/4 *teaspoon lemon juice*

1. Preheat the oven to 200 degrees or slightly lower if possible. Brush a large baking sheet with melted butter, and sprinkle with flour. Tip the pan to coat evenly; then tap out the excess.

2. Place the egg whites in the small bowl of an electric mixer, and start beating at low speed. When soft peaks form, increase the speed to high, and gradually beat in about half the sugar (if the sugar is not added slowly enough, the meringues will be granular). Gradually add the remaining sugar alternately with the lemon juice, beating until the sugar is completely dissolved (test with the fingers). The meringue should be stiff and glossy.

3. Spoon the meringue into a pastry bag fitted with a round-tipped No. 8 pastry tube.

4. Press the meringue into twelve ovals onto the prepared pan. They should be 3 to 3 1/2 inches long and 1 1/2 to 2 inches wide and spaced about 1 1/2 inches apart.

5. Bake the meringues for about 2 to 2 1/2 hours, or until dried and crisp. (They should be white, not cream-colored, the reason for using such a low heat; in fact, the meringues are not actually baked, simply dried.) Remove the pan from the oven, and cool. Store loosely in a covered container (not airtight) at room temperature until ready to use. They will keep for weeks if that is desired.

COGNAC CHOCOLATE SAUCE

6 tablespoons sugar
3/4 cup water
3 ounces semisweet chocolate
3 ounces unsweetened chocolate
3 tablespoons unsalted butter, cut into chunks
1 tablespoon cognac or brandy

1. Combine the sugar and water in a 1-quart saucepan. Set over high heat, and stir until the sugar dissolves and heavy

bubbles appear around the edge. Cover and reduce the heat to low. Simmer for 5 minutes; uncover, remove from the heat, and cool to lukewarm.

2. Chop the chocolates into coarse pieces, and melt with the butter in a small, heavy saucepan set over very low heat. Stir occasionally until the chocolate is melted and the mixture is smooth. Remove from the heat.

3. Gradually stir the lukewarm sugar syrup into the chocolate mixture. Blend in the cognac. Cover and store at a warm room temperature until lukewarm and ready to serve. (It should be slightly thickened but pourable.) If held too long, it may be necessary to reheat briefly to bring to a pouring consistency.

Note: The sauce keeps well overnight or longer at room temperature but will need to be reheated. Do not refrigerate, or it will harden.

BROWNIE SUNDAES

One of America's favorite bar cookies here turned into a special dessert: a square of moist Brownie, topped with a scoop of vanilla ice cream, smothered in pecan chocolate sauce. The dessert serves 12, but the component parts can stand alone and be served individually.

4 ounces unsweetened chocolate, chopped into coarse pieces
1 cup (2 sticks) unsalted butter, softened
1 pound confectioners' sugar
1/2 teaspoon salt
4 large eggs, at room temperature
2 teaspoons vanilla extract
1 1/2 cups sifted all-purpose flour
About 1 1/2 pints vanilla ice cream
Milk Chocolate Pecan Sauce (recipe follows)

1. Line the bottom and sides of a $9 \times 12 \times 2$-inch baking pan with foil. (To do this easily, invert the pan, and press the foil smoothly over the top and sides. Remove; then insert into the pan, and press into shape.) Brush the foil with melted shortening. Preheat the oven to 350 degrees, placing a rack one-third up from the bottom.

2. Melt the chocolate in the top of a double boiler set over hot water. Set aside to cool slightly.

3. In the large bowl of an electric mixer cream the butter. Gradually add the sugar and salt; then continue beating until light and fluffy. Beat in first the eggs, two at a time, then the vanilla, and then the chocolate, beating after each addition only until smoothly blended. Add the flour, and beat at low speed just long enough to incorporate.

4. Turn the batter into the prepared baking pan, spreading it evenly. Bake for about 35 minutes, reversing the pan from front to back if necessary (toward the end) to ensure even

baking. There will be a thick, crisp crust on top, and the center, when tested with a wooden pick, will be moist.

5. Remove the pan from the oven, and cool to room temperature on a rack. Cover securely with plastic wrap or foil to keep moist.

6. When ready to serve, invert the brownies onto a cookie sheet, and remove the wrap. Cover with a second cookie sheet, and invert again, leaving the crust side up. Cut into twelve 3-inch squares, using a sharp long knife. Place the squares on individual serving plates. Top each with a small scoop of ice cream; then spoon a generous portion of the warm chocolate sauce over each. Serve immediately.

MAKES 12 GENEROUS SERVINGS.

MILK CHOCOLATE PECAN SAUCE

12 ounces milk chocolate, chopped into coarse pieces
1 1/2 cups light cream
3 tablespoons brandy
3/4 cup pecans, chopped into coarse pieces

1. Place the chocolate in the top of a double boiler, and set over warm water to melt; stir frequently (it must be melted slowly, or it may lump). Gradually add the cream, and stir until smooth.

2. Remove the pan from the hot water, and place over direct heat at a medium-low temperature. Cook, stirring constantly, for 4 to 5 minutes, or until the sauce thickens slightly. Remove from the heat, and stir in the brandy and pecans.

3. Use immediately, or keep warm over hot water; or let cool and reheat slowly over direct heat when ready to serve.

ICE CREAM SANDWICHES

A simple frozen treat made with packaged plain chocolate wafers. A child's delight.

1 large egg white, at room temperature
6 tablespoons sugar
1 cup heavy cream
1 tablespoon instant coffee powder
1 teaspoon vanilla extract
40 thin chocolate wafers*
About 1 cup fine-chopped toasted almonds (page 20)

1. Beat the egg white with a wire whisk until soft peaks form. Gradually whisk in 2 tablespoons of the sugar, beating until stiff.

2. In a separate bowl combine the cream and the remaining 4 tablespoons sugar, the coffee powder, and the vanilla. Beat until the mixture forms soft peaks; then fold in the egg white.

3. Place a dollop of the mixture, about 2 tablespoons, onto the flat side of half the chocolate wafers. Top with the remaining wafers, and press lightly so that the filling comes to the edges. Place each sandwich as filled in a pan large enough to accommodate the sandwiches in a single layer. Freeze until the filling is firm.

4. Spread the chopped almonds in a thin layer on a sheet of wax paper. Then, holding one sandwich in your fingers like a wheel, run the edges through the nuts to coat lightly. Repeat with the remaining filled cookies. Freeze again for several hours or overnight, or until ready to serve. (If the sandwiches are held longer, wrap them individually in foil or plastic wrap to seal out the air.)

MAKES 20 SANDWICHES.

*The chocolate wafers required are the Nabisco brand; each 8 1/2-ounce package contains about 40 cookies.

SYDNEY'S MARK III

A triple-layer frozen dessert: chocolate crumb crust, buttery chocolate cream, and coffee ice cream with a garnish of salty pecans.

CHOCOLATE CRUMB CRUST

1 1/2 cups chocolate wafer crumbs
3 tablespoons unsalted butter, melted

CHOCOLATE FILLING

2 ounces semisweet chocolate
1/2 cup (1 stick) unsalted butter, softened
1 teaspoon vanilla extract
2 cups confectioners' sugar, sifted
3 eggs, at room temperature

ICE CREAM FILLING AND GARNISH

2 pints coffee ice cream
Salted toasted pecans, for garnish*

1. *For the crust:* Combine the crumbs and butter. Press firmly onto the bottom of a 9-inch springform pan (sides attached). Refrigerate while preparing the chocolate filling.

*Salted toasted pecans: Melt about 1 teaspoon or more of unsalted butter in a small skillet to coat the bottom lightly. Add 3/4 cup pecan halves, and sprinkle with 1/4 teaspoon coarse salt. Stir over low heat until the pecans are lightly toasted. Turn out onto paper toweling to cool before using them.

2. *For the chocolate filling:* Chop the chocolate into course pieces; then melt slowly in a small, heavy saucepan, stirring occasionally. Remove from the heat and cool slightly.

In a small mixing bowl, with electric beaters, cream the butter with the vanilla until light and smooth. Add the sugar; beat until creamy. Then blend in the melted chocolate.

Add the eggs to the chocolate mixture, one at a time, beating on medium speed after each addition until thoroughly blended. After the last egg has been added, beat for 2 to 3 minutes longer. The idea is to incorporate as much air as possible.

Turn the mixture onto the chilled crust, spreading to make an even layer. Freeze for at least 30 minutes, or until firm.

3. *For the ice cream filling:* Place the ice cream cartons in the refrigerator just long enough to soften slightly. Then turn the ice cream into a chilled bowl, and whip with a fork just until smooth. Spread it evenly over the top of the chocolate mixture, and garnish the top with the pecans, rounded sides up, pressing them in slightly. Cover the top airtight with foil, and return to the freezer. Freeze for at least 4 hours, or until firm, or up to several days.

4. To serve, remove the sides of the springform pan. Cut the frozen dessert into wedges, allowing it to soften slightly if necessary. Place, cut sides down, on individual dessert plates, and serve immediately.

MAKES 10 TO 12 SERVINGS.

GRAND MARNIER CHOCOLATE MOUSSE TORTE

Chocolate cookie crumbs form the crust to enrich this easily made and delectable mousse filling. The orange liqueur-flavored whipped cream topping and a special chocolate garnish bring it to perfection.

CHOCOLATE CRUMB CRUST

1 1/2 cups (about 6 ounces) chocolate wafer crumbs
1/2 cup (1 stick) unsalted butter, melted

MOUSSE FILLING

16 ounces semisweet chocolate, chopped into coarse pieces
6 large eggs, at room temperature
1/4 cup Grand Marnier or other orange-flavored liqueur
2 cups heavy cream
1/4 teaspoon salt

TOPPING

1 cup heavy cream
1 tablespoon Grand Marnier
Chocolate scrolls (page 11)

1. *For the crust:* Combine the crumbs and butter, mixing well with a fork. Press onto the bottom and sides of an ungreased 8 × 3-inch springform pan. The mixture should be pressed evenly and come to the top of the pan. Refrigerate while preparing the filling.

2. *For the mousse filling:* Melt the chocolate in a large metal mixing bowl set over a saucepan of barely simmering water (or use a double boiler). Stir occasionally as the chocolate melts, and when it is smooth, remove it from over the water, and cool it to lukewarm.

Add 2 whole eggs and 2 egg yolks to the chocolate. Using a wire whisk, stir briskly to blend well. Add the Grand Marnier, and continue stirring until the mixture is smooth and creamy.

Whip the cream until almost stiff. Beat the remaining 4 egg whites with the salt until stiff but not dry. Stir a little of each of the cream and the egg whites into the chocolate mixture to lighten it; then alternately fold in the remaining whites and whipped cream in two or three additions each. Turn into the prepared crust, and shake slightly to level. Freeze the torte until the filling is firm enough so that the topping can be spread over the top.

3. *For the topping:* Whip the cream until soft peaks form; gradually beat in the Grand Marnier, and continue beating until fairly stiff. Spread smoothly over the chilled filling. Return the torte to the freezer, and freeze for at least 24 hours, or until ready to serve, or for several days if preferred.

4. To serve, run a sharp knife around the edges of the torte pan to release the crust; then remove the sides. Garnish with the chocolate scrolls to cover the top. Serve immediately while the torte is frozen.

MAKES 12 TO 14 SERVINGS.

WHITE CHOCOLATE MOUSSE TART

A golden mousse filling made with white chocolate set in a bittersweet chocolate crumb crust. An unusual frozen delight.

> *Bittersweet Chocolate Crumb Crust (recipe follows)*
> *4 ounces white chocolate, chopped into coarse pieces*
> *1/2 cup (1 stick) unsalted butter, cut into small pieces*
> *3 eggs, separated, at room temperature*
> *1/8 teaspoon salt*
> *1/4 cup sugar*

1. Prepare the crust as directed.

2. Place the chocolate in a heatproof mixing bowl, and set over a saucepan partially filled with water (do not allow the bowl to touch the water). Bring the water to a simmer. When the chocolate starts to melt, add the butter. Stir until well blended (the butter will separate); then remove the bowl from the heat. Add the egg yolks; beat with a whisk just until thoroughly blended and creamy.

3. Place the bowl briefly in the refrigerator for about 5 minutes, or until the mixture is slightly cooler than lukewarm. (Take care not to overchill because it will harden.)

4. Beat the egg whites with the salt until they form soft peaks. Gradually add the sugar, beating briskly until the mixture is stiff. Stir a tablespoon or two of the egg whites into the white chocolate mixture; then fold in the remainder.

5. Turn the mixture into the prepared crust, spreading it evenly. Sprinkle the remaining chocolate crumbs over the top. Freeze for at least 8 hours, or until firm, or overnight if desired. When ready to serve, let stand for 10 minutes at room temperature before cutting the tart into wedges.

MAKES 8 SERVINGS.

BITTERSWEET CHOCOLATE CRUMB CRUST

1/4 cup (1/2 stick) unsalted butter, melted
1/2 ounce unsweetened chocolate
1 1/2 cups chocolate wafer crumbs

Melt the butter with the chocolate in a small saucepan set over very low heat. Remove from the heat, and mix in the wafer crumbs. Reserve 2 tablespoons of the crumbs for garnish. Press the remainder firmly and evenly onto the bottom and sides of an ungreased 9-inch pie plate. Refrigerate until firm.

FROZEN CHOCOLATE CHEESE PIE

Just enough cream cheese to give the filling tang and a spare amount of chocolate to color and flavor it lightly.

Graham Cracker Crumb Crust (recipe follows)
8 ounces cream cheese, softened
2 large eggs, at room temperature
1/2 cup sugar
1 teaspoon vanilla extract
6 ounces semisweet chocolate, melted and cooled
1 1/2 cups heavy cream
1 tablespoon confectioners' sugar, mixed with 1 teaspoon
   unsweetened cocoa powder, for garnish

1. Prepare and chill the crumb crust as directed.
2. Place the cream cheese, eggs, sugar, and vanilla in the bowl of an electric mixer. (It is important that the cheese and eggs be at room temperature, or the mixture will not blend smoothly.) Start beating at low speed, and when it is well blended, add the chocolate; then increase the speed to high. Continue beating until the mixture is light and smooth.
3. In a separate bowl beat the heavy cream until thick but not buttery. Fold about two-thirds of the whipped cream by hand into the chocolate mixture, leaving about 1 cup in the bowl for topping (refrigerate this portion).
4. Turn the chocolate mixture into the chilled crust, spreading it evenly. Freeze for about 1 hour, or until fairly firm.
5. When the filling is firm, whip the chilled cream briefly, if necessary, to incorporate any liquid at the bottom of the bowl. Spread the cream over the filling, swirling it decoratively. Freeze for at least 24 hours, or until solid, or for several days, if preferred.
6. When ready to serve, remove the dessert from the

freezer, and let it stand just long enough so that the crust can be cut through easily, about 10 minutes.

7. Just before serving, dust a little of the confectioners' sugar mixture lightly over the top; then cut into wedges.

MAKES 8 SERVINGS.

GRAHAM CRACKER CRUMB CRUST

1 1/3 cups graham cracker crumbs
3 tablespoons sugar
1 tablespoon unsweetened cocoa powder
5 tablespoons unsalted butter, melted

Combine the crumbs, sugar, and cocoa in a small bowl, using the back of a spoon to crush any lumps of sugar or cocoa. Add the melted butter, mixing with a fork until evenly distributed. Pour into an ungreased 9-inch pie plate, and press the mixture evenly and firmly with the back of a spoon to cover the bottom and the sides (not the rim). Bake in a preheated 350-degree oven for 8 to 10 minutes. Set on a rack to cool slightly; then refrigerate or freeze until cold.

BLACK BOTTOM LEMON CURD PIE

A perfectly matched combination of flavors: lemon and chocolate. The crumb crust is made with chocolate wafers; the citrus filling combines layers of vanilla ice cream and tart lemon curd.

> **Chocolate Crumb Crust (recipe follows)**
> **1/4 cup (1/2 stick) unsalted butter**
> **1/3 cup (about 2 large lemons) fresh lemon juice**
> **Grated zest of 1 large lemon**
> **3/4 cup sugar**
> **1/8 teaspoon salt**
> **3 large eggs, at room temperature**
> **1 pint vanilla ice cream**
> **Candied Lemon Peel (page 18), for optional garnish**

1. Prepare the crust, reserving the crumbs required for garnish. Freeze while preparing the filling.

2. Melt the butter in a medium-size, heavy saucepan. Stir in the lemon juice and zest, sugar, and salt. Cook, stirring, until the sugar is dissolved; remove from the heat.

3. Beat the eggs slightly in a small mixing bowl. Gradually blend in the lemon juice mixture; then return to the saucepan. Cook over low heat, stirring for about 2 to 3 minutes, or until the mixture thickens. Do not allow it to come to a boil. Remove from the heat, and chill for at least 30 minutes, or until cold.

4. Place the ice cream in the refrigerator just long enough to make it spreadable. Then spread half over the bottom of the chocolate crumb crust. Cover that with slightly less than half the lemon curd. Repeat the layers. Sprinkle the top with the reserved chocolate crumbs. Freeze the pie for about 4 to 6 hours, or until solidly frozen, or longer, if desired.

5. When ready to serve, let stand for 10 minutes at room

temperature to soften slightly; then cut into wedges. Garnish each portion with lemon peels, if used.

MAKES 6 TO 8 SERVINGS.

CHOCOLATE CRUMB CRUST

1 1/2 cups chocolate wafer crumbs
1/4 cup (1/2 stick) unsalted butter, melted

Combine the cookie crumbs and butter. Reserve 1 tablespoon for garnish. Press the remainder firmly and evenly onto the bottom and sides (just to the rim) of an ungreased 9-inch pie plate. Bake for 8 minutes in a preheated 350-degree oven. Cool completely; then freeze while preparing the filling.

PEANUT BUTTER CRUNCH PIE

This unusual cheesecake pie is served with a hot fudge sauce.

> *Chocolate Crumb Crust (recipe follows)*
> *6 ounces cream cheese, softened*
> *3/4 cup chunky-style peanut butter*
> *1 cup confectioners' sugar, sifted*
> *1/4 teaspoon salt*
> *1/2 cup milk*
> *1/2 teaspoon vanilla extract*
> *1 1/2 cups heavy cream*
> *Hot Fudge Sauce (recipe follows)*

1. Prepare the crust as directed, and refrigerate or freeze it until cold.

2. In the large bowl of an electric mixer beat the cream cheese, peanut butter, sugar, and salt until well blended and smooth. Gradually blend in first the milk, then the vanilla; continue beating until creamy.

3. In a separate bowl beat the cream until soft peaks form. Fold into the peanut butter mixture. Turn into the prepared crust, spreading it smoothly so that it mounds slightly. Freeze for at least 4 hours, or until firm.

4. When ready to serve, cut the pie into wedges, and spoon a little of the hot chocolate sauce over each serving.

Note: If the pie filling is solidly frozen, allow it to stand at room temperature until it will cut through easily; the consistency should be that of creamy ice cream.

MAKES 8 TO 10 SERVINGS.

CHOCOLATE CRUMB CRUST

1 1/2 cups chocolate wafer crumbs
1/4 cup (1/2 stick) unsalted butter, melted

Combine the cookie crumbs and butter, using a fork to mix them evenly. Press the mixture firmly and evenly onto the bottom and sides (just to the rim) of an ungreased 9-inch pie plate. Bake in a preheated 350-degree oven for 8 minutes; remove from the oven, and cool completely on a rack before filling.

HOT FUDGE SAUCE

2 ounces unsweetened chocolate, chopped into coarse pieces
1/4 cup (1/2 stick) unsalted butter
2/3 cup heavy cream
2 cups sifted confectioners' sugar

1. Combine the chocolate, butter, and cream in a 1 1/2-quart heavy saucepan with a tight-fitting lid. Cook, stirring constantly, over very low heat until the chocolate dissolves and the mixture comes to a boil. (Cooking over a very low heat is the secret of a smooth sauce.)

2. Blend in the sugar; bring to a boil, stirring constantly. Then cover the pan, and allow the mixture to boil for 3 minutes; remove from the heat, and allow to cool slightly, but serve hot.

Note: The sauce may be prepared ahead, covered, and refrigerated. Reheat to boiling before using.

VII
HOT DESSERTS

CLASSIC FRENCH CHOCOLATE SOUFFLÉ
CHOCOLATE FOAM SOUFFLÉS
CHOCOLATE FONDUE SOUFFLÉ
CINNAMON CHOCOLATE BREAD PUDDINGS
STEAMED CHOCOLATE PUDDING
WITH RUM SAUCE
MOOR IN HIS SHIRT

CLASSIC FRENCH CHOCOLATE SOUFFLÉ

The French chef's pride: an airy soufflé baked just long enough so that the outside is gently firm, with the center still warm and creamy, so that it can be served as a token sauce.

6 tablespoons sugar
2 tablespoons flour
1 cup milk
1 tablespoon unsalted butter
2 ounces unsweetened chocolate, chopped into coarse pieces
1 teaspoon vanilla extract
3 large eggs, separated, at room temperature
1/8 teaspoon salt
1 or 2 sugar tablets, for optional garnish

1. Grease only the bottom of a 1-quart soufflé dish (a ceramic dish with a flat bottom and straight sides). Preheat the oven to 325 degrees.

2. Combine the sugar and flour in a small, heavy saucepan. Blend in the milk; then add the butter and chocolate. Cook over low heat, stirring constantly, until the mixture is thickened and smooth. Remove from the heat, and stir in the vanilla. Set aside to cool slightly.

3. In a large mixing bowl beat the egg yolks until very light and slightly thickened. Gradually fold in the chocolate mixture.

4. Beat the egg whites with the salt until stiff but still moist peaks form. Gently fold them into the chocolate mixture. (A few patches of white may show through the mixture.)

5. Turn the soufflé mixture into the soufflé dish, spreading it evenly. Bake for 30 minutes. At this point the top should be firm, the inside soft enough to serve as a sauce. If the optional sugar garnish is used, crush the tablets, and sprinkle over the top during the last 5 minutes of baking. Serve immediately.

6. To serve, divide the soufflé into serving portions by holding two large spoons held back to back. Then spoon out onto serving plates, adding a little of the uncooked center to each for sauce.

MAKES 4 SERVINGS.

CHOCOLATE FOAM SOUFFLÉS

Perfect individual soufflés, lighter than those made with flour and butter, and easier to make. The mixture rises high in the soufflé dish, forming a rounded dome that makes an impressive presentation. A simple dusting of powdered sugar covers the dome.

3 ounces semisweet chocolate
1 ounce unsweetened chocolate
1/2 cup sugar
2 tablespoons Kahlúa or other coffee-flavored liqueur
8 large eggs, separated, at room temperature
Confectioners' sugar, for garnish

1. Grease generously four individual 1 1/2-cup soufflé dishes, and have ready a cookie sheet on which to bake the soufflés. Preheat the oven to 425 degrees, setting a rack in the center.

2. Chop the chocolates into coarse pieces. Place in a large mixing bowl, and set over hot water. Stir occasionally until the chocolate is melted. Remove the bowl, and blend in 1/4 cup of the sugar and the liqueur; cool slightly. One by one, add the egg yolks, and beat until thoroughly blended. Set aside.

3. In a separate bowl whip the egg whites until they form soft peaks. Then gradually beat in the remaining 1/4 cup sugar, and continue beating until stiff.

4. Using a wire whisk, quickly but gently beat about half the egg whites into the chocolate mixture, just until the mixture is lightened. Then fold in the remainder of the egg whites with a rubber spatula until no white traces remain.

5. Turn the soufflé mixture into the prepared dishes, dividing it equally. (The mixture will come to the tops.)

6. Immediately place the dishes on the cookie sheet, and bake for 10 to 12 minutes, or until the soufflés rise high above

the dishes into rounded domes and the tops show a light crust. Remove from the oven, dust the tops lightly with confectioners' sugar (put through a wire sieve), place on dessert plates, and serve immediately.

MAKES 4 GENEROUS SERVINGS.

CHOCOLATE FONDUE SOUFFLÉ

Denser than the usual soufflé, this one rises only slightly in the baking.

2 ounces unsweetened chocolate, chopped into coarse pieces
2 cups milk
1/2 cup sugar
3 tablespoons flour
1/2 teaspoon salt
2 tablespoons unsalted butter
1 teaspoon vanilla extract
3 eggs, separated, at room temperature
2 cups soft breadcrumbs*
Sweetened Whipped Cream (recipe follows)

1. Grease a 1 1/2-quart baking dish (it need not be a straight-sided soufflé dish). Preheat the oven to 350 degrees.

2. Combine the chocolate and milk in a medium-size saucepan. Set over low heat, and stir until the chocolate is melted; then remove from the heat. (The mixture will appear grainy but will smooth out in the next process.)

3. Combine the sugar, flour, and salt in a small mixing bowl. Gradually blend in part of the milk mixture; then return to the saucepan. Continue to cook over low heat, stirring constantly, until the mixture thickens and comes to a boil. Boil for 1 minute. Remove from the heat, and stir in first the butter, then the vanilla.

4. Beat the egg yolks slightly. Stir in a little of the hot milk mixture; then blend into the remainder in the saucepan. Stir in the breadcrumbs, and set aside to cool slightly.

5. Beat the egg whites until stiff peaks form; then fold into the cooled mixture, gently but completely.

---

*To make the soft breadcrumbs required, remove the crusts from fresh sliced bread, and dice very fine. In measuring, press down lightly in the cup.

6. Turn the batter into the prepared baking dish. Set in a pan of hot water (it should come almost to the level of the batter). Bake for about 1 hour and 10 minutes, or until the top of the soufflé is puffy and dry. Remove the dish from the water, and serve immediately, with the whipped cream in a separate serving bowl.

Note: The soufflé is also delicious served at room temperature.

MAKES 6 TO 8 SERVINGS.

SWEETENED WHIPPED CREAM

1 cup heavy cream
4 tablespoons confectioners' sugar
1/2 teaspoon vanilla extract

Whip the cream with the sugar and vanilla until the mixture mounds softly. Serve immediately.

CINNAMON CHOCOLATE BREAD PUDDINGS

A simple, economical dessert that is easy to make. It's like no bread pudding you've ever tried before. Serve it hot, lukewarm, or cold; the pudding is a delight.

6 ounces semisweet chocolate, chopped into coarse pieces
1/2 cup granulated sugar
1/4 teaspoon salt
1/2 teaspoon ground cinnamon
2 1/2 cups soft fresh bread cubes*
1 1/2 cups milk
1 egg, at room temperature
Confectioners' sugar, as garnish

1. Grease six individual 1-cup soufflé dishes, and place on a baking sheet. Preheat the oven to 400 degrees, setting a rack in the middle.

2. Melt the chocolate in a large mixing bowl set over a saucepan containing barely simmering water. Stir the chocolate occasionally, and when it is melted, remove the bowl from the water. Add the granulated sugar, salt, cinnamon, and bread cubes. Gradually stir in the milk; then add the egg. Using a wire whisk, beat the ingredients vigorously just until well blended.

3. Spoon or carefully pour the mixture into the soufflé dishes (they will be only slightly more than half filled, and the mixture will barely rise during baking; nonetheless it is important to use 1-cup soufflé dishes to ensure proper baking). Bake for 15 minutes, or until the tops are barely firm to the touch.

*To make the bread cubes, remove the crusts (if crisp) from fresh sliced bread, and cut the bread into small cubes. In measuring, press down lightly. Ideally thin-sliced bread, such as the Pepperidge Farm or Arnold brand, should be used since it is firm and thin enough for proper cutting and the crusts are soft enough to eliminate trimming.

4. Allow the puddings to cool for at least 10 minutes before serving; then dust the tops lightly with confectioners' sugar. (Alternately the puddings may be served warm or close to room temperature.)

Note: The centers of the puddings are intentionally underbaked, forming a sauce that is thin when the puddings are first served and gradually thickens as they cool. At any stage of presentation they are delicious.

MAKES 6 SERVINGS.

STEAMED CHOCOLATE PUDDING
WITH RUM SAUCE

When steamed, this pudding tastes like a rich chocolate cake. It is served warm with a fluffy rum-flavored sauce.

1/3 cup unsalted butter, softened
1 cup sugar
1 teaspoon vanilla extract
1 egg, at room temperature
2 ounces unsweetened chocolate, melted and cooled
1 1/2 cups sifted all-purpose flour
1 teaspoon baking soda
1/4 teaspoon salt
1 1/4 cups milk
Rum Sauce (recipe follows)

1. Grease well, then flour a 1 1/2-quart pudding mold or mixing bowl. Have ready a steamer containing a rack or a kettle inserted with a rack, either with a tight-fitting lid.

2. Using a wooden spoon, cream the 1/3 cup butter and sugar until well blended. Add the vanilla and the egg; beat well to incorporate; then blend in the cooled melted chocolate.

3. Sift together the flour, baking soda, and salt. Add to the creamed mixture alternately with the milk, beating just until smooth.

4. Pour the mixture into the pudding mold. Cover tightly with a sheet of foil, and place on the rack over boiling water. Cover the pan with a lid. Set the steamer over medium-high heat, and steam for 1 hour, or until the pudding tests done with a wooden pick inserted in the center. (Replenish the boiling water as needed.)

5. Remove the mold, and let it stand, uncovered, on a rack for 10 minutes. To unmold the pudding, loosen the edges with a thin spatula, and shake gently to be sure that it is com-

ing away from the sides. Place a serving plate over the mold, invert, and remove the mold carefully. Serve warm with the rum sauce, passed separately.

MAKES 8 TO 10 SERVINGS.

RUM SAUCE

3 eggs, separated, at room temperature
1 1/2 cups confectioners' sugar, sifted
3/4 cup heavy cream
1 1/2 tablespoons light or dark rum
1/4 teaspoon salt

In a small mixing bowl, with a wire whisk, beat the egg yolks until light. Gradually whisk in the sugar; blend in the rum. Beat the cream in a chilled large bowl with electric beaters until it mounds softly. Fold in the egg yolk mixture. Whip the egg whites with the salt until stiff but not dry. Fold into the whipped cream mixture. Serve immediately.

Note: The egg yolk and whipped cream mixture may be refrigerated for several hours. If it begins to separate, whisk it lightly; then fold in the beaten egg whites.

MOOR IN HIS SHIRT

In Austria where this delicate dessert originated, it is called Mohr im Hemd. *The dessert is baked in individual servings, unmolded, then topped with hot bittersweet chocolate sauce and garnished with a token amount of whipped cream.*

> *1/2 cup (1 stick) unsalted butter, softened*
> *4 tablespoons confectioners' sugar, sifted*
> *1 teaspoon vanilla extract*
> *6 large eggs, separated, at room temperature*
> *4 ounces semisweet chocolate, grated (page 9)*
> *3/4 cup ground toasted almonds (page 20)*
> *1/4 teaspoon salt*
> *3 tablespoons granulated sugar*
> *Hot Chocolate Sauce (recipe follows)*
> *Whipped Cream (recipe follows)*

1. You will need eight 1/2-cup molds, such as small soufflé dishes or custard cups. Grease the bottoms and sides with softened unsalted butter; then coat with granulated sugar, tapping out the excess. Place in a deep roasting pan; set aside. Preheat the oven to 350 degrees, setting a rack in the center.

2. In the bowl of an electric mixer cream the 1/2 cup butter with the confectioners' sugar; then beat until light and fluffy. Blend in the vanilla. Add the egg yolks, one at a time, beating until thoroughly incorporated after each addition.

3. Using a rubber spatula, blend in the grated chocolate and almonds. Mix just until blended.

4. In a separate mixer bowl beat the egg whites with the salt until they hold soft peaks; gradually beat in the 3 tablespoons granulated sugar, and continue beating until the meringue is glossy and will hold a stiff peak. Stir one-third of the meringue into the chocolate mixture to lighten it; then fold in the remainder until no white traces remain.

5. Spoon the batter into the prepared molds, dividing it evenly. They will be filled almost to the top. Shake lightly to level. Pour hot water into the pan until it reaches halfway up the sides of the molds. Bake for 35 to 40 minutes, or until the puddings have puffed slightly and are barely springy to the touch.

6. Carefully unmold the puddings while hot. Run the tip of a sharp knife around the top edge to release; then invert onto individual dessert plates. Spoon the hot sauce over the tops to cover completely. Place a spoonful of the whipped cream at the side of each, and serve immediately.

Note: The puddings are also delicious served when barely warm. Add the sauce when ready to serve.

MAKES 8 SERVINGS.

HOT CHOCOLATE SAUCE

2 ounces unsweetened chocolate, chopped into coarse pieces
6 tablespoons water
1/2 cup sugar
1/8 teaspoon salt
3 tablespoons unsalted butter
1/4 teaspoon vanilla extract

Combine the chocolate and water in a medium-size, heavy saucepan. Set over low heat, and stir until smooth. Add the sugar and salt; continue to cook, stirring, until the mixture is smooth and slightly thickened. Add the butter, and stir until blended. Remove from the heat; let cool for a few minutes; then stir in the vanilla. Use immediately, or keep hot over a saucepan of warm water. (If preferred, make several hours in advance and reheat when necessary; if desired, this sauce may be kept in the refrigerator for many weeks.)

WHIPPED CREAM

1/2 cup heavy cream
1 tablespoon confectioners' sugar
1/8 teaspoon vanilla extract

Whip the cream, sugar, and vanilla in a chilled bowl with chilled beaters. It should be fairly stiff, but do not overbeat.

VIII

PIES AND TARTS

PECAN FUDGE PIE

FUDGE PUDDING PIE

CAROLINA CHOCOLATE CHESS TART

NORWEGIAN FUDGE TART

CHERRY CHOCOLATE CREAM PIE

BROWN DERBY PIE

NEWPORT CUSTARD PIE WITH CHOCOLATE GLAZE

CHOCOLATE CHIFFON PIE

COCOA ALMOND PARTY PIE

PINK PEPPERMINT PIE WITH CHOCOLATE ICING

BRANDY ALEXANDER PIE

PECAN FUDGE PIE

As its name suggests, this dessert is a combination of two beloved pies: pecan and fudge. It is chocolaty, rich, and dense and is best served in small portions with a generous spoonful of whipped cream on the side.

> *1 unbaked 9-inch Flaky Pastry Shell (recipe follows)*
> *3 ounces unsweetened chocolate*
> *1/2 cup (1 stick) unsalted butter*
> *4 eggs, at room temperature*
> *1 1/2 cups sugar*
> *3 tablespoons dark corn syrup*
> *1 teaspoon vanilla extract*
> *1/4 teaspoon salt*
> *1 cup pecan halves*
> *Whipped Cream (recipe follows)*

1. Prepare the pastry shell, using a high, fluted edge, as directed. Preheat the oven to 350 degrees.

2. Chop the chocolate into coarse pieces, and place with the butter, cut into chunks, in a small, heavy saucepan. Set over low heat until partially melted; then remove from the heat, and stir until the two ingredients are completely melted and smooth. Set aside.

3. In a large mixing bowl, with a wire whisk or electric beater, beat the eggs slightly. Beat in the sugar, corn syrup, vanilla, and salt just long enough to blend. Stir in first the chocolate mixture, then the pecans.

4. Pour the filling into the prepared pastry shell. Bake for 45 to 50 minutes, or until the filling is firmly set around the edges and a wooden pick comes out clean when inserted halfway to the center. The center should seem slightly underdone; shake the pie plate slightly to test. Remove from the oven, and set on a rack to cool. The filling will rise as it bakes, and may even crack, but will settle as it cools.

5. Serve the pie at room temperature with the whipped cream passed separately. Do not be tempted to serve the pie warm, for the filling is soft and must be cooled in order to firm.

MAKES 10 SERVINGS.

FLAKY PASTRY SHELL

This pastry may be used for either an 8- or 9-inch pie and used unbaked or prebaked.

>   1 cup plus 2 tablespoons sifted all-purpose flour
>   1/2 teaspoon salt
>   6 tablespoons vegetable shortening
>   2 1/2 to 3 tablespoons cold water

1. Sift the flour and salt together into a mixing bowl. Cut in half the shortening with a pastry blender until it looks like coarse meal; cut in the remainder of the shortening until it is the size of small peas.

2. Sprinkle the cold water over the mixture, a scant tablespoon at a time, mixing lightly with a fork until all the flour is moistened and the dough barely clings together. (Use a minimum amount of water; too much will make the dough sticky.) Gather the dough together with lightly floured hands; then pat lightly to flatten.

3. Roll out the dough on a lightly floured board to a 1/8-inch thickness (about 1 1/2 inches larger in diameter than an inverted 9-inch pie plate, 2 inches larger than an inverted 8-inch pie plate).

4. Transfer to the ungreased pie plate; trim the edges to a 1/2-inch overhang; then fold under and flute the edges with your fingers, or press the edge flat with the tines of a fork. Bake as directed for the filling used.

Baked pastry shell: Prick the pastry thoroughly with a fork to prevent puffing during baking. Bake in a preheated 400-degree oven for 10 to 12 minutes, or until golden brown. Check after 5 minutes. If the pastry puffs in the center, prick again two or three times to release the air. Cool on a rack.

WHIPPED CREAM

2 cups heavy cream
2 tablespoons confectioners' sugar
1 teaspoon vanilla extract

Whip the cream with the sugar and vanilla until soft peaks form. Do not overbeat; it should be fluffy, not stiff.

FUDGE PUDDING PIE

This is pie, pudding, and cake combined into one dessert. It is served warm, topped with whipped cream or ice cream.

1 unbaked 9-inch Flaky Pastry Shell (page 196)
2 ounces unsweetened chocolate, chopped into coarse pieces
1 tablespoon unsalted butter
3/4 cup sifted all-purpose flour
1 1/4 cups sugar
1 1/2 teaspoons baking powder
1/4 teaspoon salt
1/3 cup chopped pecans
1/3 cup milk
1/2 teaspoon vanilla extract
1 ounce unsweetened chocolate, grated (page 9)
1 cup boiling water
Whipped cream or vanilla ice cream

1. Prepare the unbaked pastry shell as directed. Preheat the oven to 375 degrees, setting a rack in the middle.

2. Melt the chopped chocolate with the butter in a small saucepan set over very low heat; set aside to cool.

3. Sift the flour, 3/4 cup of the sugar, baking powder, and salt together into a mixing bowl. Add the pecans, milk and vanilla; mix just until blended. Blend in the melted chocolate and butter mixture. Turn into the unbaked pastry shell, spreading it as evenly as possible with a wet spatula.

4. Combine the grated chocolate with the remaining 1/2 cup sugar, and sprinkle evenly over the filling. Pour the boiling water over the top; do not stir in.

5. Bake the pie for 35 to 40 minutes, or until the filling is set except for the center; it will firm upon cooling. Cool on

a rack to nearly room temperature; then cut into wedges for serving. Serve warm with whipped cream or a small scoop of vanilla ice cream.

Note: If baked in advance, reheat briefly in a warm oven.

MAKES 8 SERVINGS.

CAROLINA CHOCOLATE CHESS TART

Chess pie, a southern favorite, is typically made with eggs and lots of butter. This tart contains melted chocolate as well.

1 unbaked 8-inch Flaky Pastry Shell (page 196)*
1/2 cup (1 stick) unsalted butter
1 ounce unsweetened chocolate, chopped into coarse pieces
2 eggs, at room temperature
1 cup granulated sugar
1 teaspoon vanilla extract
Confectioners' sugar, for garnish

1. Prepare the pastry for the pie filling as directed; press the edges decoratively with the tines of a fork to flatten. Preheat the oven to 325 degrees, setting a rack in the center.

2. Melt the butter with the chocolate in a small saucepan set over very low heat. Set aside to cool.

3. Using a wire whisk, beat the eggs slightly in a mixing bowl. Add the granulated sugar and vanilla; whisk briefly until mixed; then blend in the chocolate mixture, and beat well to incorporate.

4. Pour the mixture into the prepared pastry shell. Bake for 30 to 35 minutes, or until the filling is set and a thin crust forms over the top. (It will rise as it bakes but settle as the pie cools.)

5. Cool the pie until barely warm, or serve at room temperature. Just before serving, dust the top with confectioners' sugar put through a wire sieve.

MAKES 6 SERVINGS.

*An 8-inch fluted tart pan with a removable bottom may be substituted. Press the pastry into the pan and against the sides, removing the excess pastry at the top edge. Remove the rim after the pie has cooled.

NORWEGIAN FUDGE TART

Unlike the previous recipes for fudge pie, the filling is prepared on top of the stove, beaten like fudge until glossy, then turned into a baked pastry shell.

1 baked 8-inch Flaky Pastry Shell (page 196)
1 cup sugar
2 tablespoons all-purpose flour
1/4 teaspoon salt
1/4 cup heavy cream
2 egg yolks, at room temperature
1 cup boiling water
2 ounces unsweetened chocolate, chopped into coarse pieces
4 tablespoons (1/2 stick) unsalted butter
1 teaspoon vanilla extract
Whipped Cream Topping (recipe follows)
Chocolate scrolls (page 11), for garnish

1. Prepare and bake the pastry shell as directed. Set aside to cool.

2. Combine the sugar, flour, and salt in a medium-size, heavy saucepan. Blend in the cream and egg yolks. Gradually add the boiling water, stirring constantly to prevent lumping.

3. Cook over low heat, stirring constantly, until the mixture thickens and comes to a full boil. Boil, stirring, for 1 minute. Remove from the heat, and add the chopped chocolate and butter. Stir until the chocolate is melted. Add the vanilla.

4. Set the saucepan in a bowl partially filled with ice water. Beat the filling with a wooden spoon until it is lukewarm, thick, and glossy like fudge. Turn into the cooled pastry shell. Refrigerate until cold and firm.

5. Prepare the whipped cream, and spread over the filling. Return to the refrigerator for up to 3 hours, but remove at least

20 minutes before serving. Cut into wedges, and top each portion with one or two chocolate scrolls.

MAKES 6 SERVINGS.

WHIPPED CREAM TOPPING

3/4 cup heavy cream
1 tablespoon confectioners' sugar
1/2 teaspoon vanilla extract

Whip the cream until almost stiff; then beat in the sugar and vanilla. Do not overbeat, or the cream may separate when spread on the pie and refrigerated.

CHERRY CHOCOLATE CREAM PIE

Dark sweet cherries in the filling; whipped cream on the top.

1 baked 9-inch Flaky Pastry Shell (page 196)
1 1/2 cups fresh dark sweet cherries*
1 1/2 cups sugar
3 tablespoons cornstarch
1/4 teaspoon salt
3 cups milk
3 ounces unsweetened chocolate, chopped into coarse pieces
3 egg yolks, at room temperature
2 tablespoons unsalted butter
1 teaspoon vanilla extract
Whipped Cream Topping (recipe follows)
Chocolate shavings (page 12), for garnish

1. Prepare the pastry shell, using a high, fluted edge, as directed. Bake and set aside to cool. Before filling, rub a teaspoon of flour over the bottom and sides of the crust. This will seal the surface and help prevent the crust from becoming soft.

2. Stem the cherries, cut in half, and remove the pits. Set aside.

3. Combine the sugar, cornstarch, and salt in a medium-size, heavy saucepan. Gradually stir in the milk. Add the chopped chocolate. Cook over medium heat, stirring constantly, until the mixture comes to a boil and is thickened and smooth. Boil, stirring, for 1 minute.

4. Beat the egg yolks slightly in a small mixing bowl; then gradually beat in about a cup of the chocolate mixture; return to the saucepan. Stir and boil for 1 minute longer. Remove from the heat and blend in the butter; cool slightly; then stir

---

*Canned cherries may be used. Drain well; then spread out onto paper toweling to absorb the remaining moisture.

in the vanilla. Cover the saucepan, and continue to cool until lukewarm but still pourable.

5. Pour a scant amount of the chocolate filling into the pastry shell (just enough to cover the bottom). Arrange the cherries in one layer over the top; then cover with the remaining filling. Press a sheet of plastic wrap onto the filling to prevent a skin from forming. Refrigerate for at least 2 hours.

6. When ready to serve, remove the plastic wrap. Prepare the whipped cream, and spread it over the filling. Garnish the top with shaved chocolate.

MAKES 6 TO 8 SERVINGS.

WHIPPED CREAM TOPPING

1 cup heavy cream
2 tablespoons confectioners' sugar
1/2 teaspoon vanilla extract

Whip the cream until slightly thickened; then beat in the sugar and vanilla. Continue beating until almost stiff. Use immediately.

BROWN DERBY PIE

This pie is a Southern specialty, a close kin to butter-rich chess pie. The butter is here, but so are chopped pecans, morsels of chocolate, and bourbon.

> 1 unbaked 9-inch Flaky Pastry Shell (page 196)
> 2 eggs, at room temperature
> 1 cup granulated sugar
> 1/2 cup sifted all-purpose flour
> 1/2 cup (1 stick) unsalted butter, melted
> 2 tablespoons bourbon
> 1 cup (6 ounces) semisweet chocolate morsels
> 1 cup fine-chopped (not ground) pecans
> Confectioners' sugar, for garnish
> Derby Whipped Cream (recipe follows)

1. Prepare the pastry for the pie filling as directed. Preheat the oven to 350 degrees.

2. Using a wire whisk, beat the eggs slightly in a mixing bowl. Add the granulated sugar, flour, melted butter, and bourbon. Beat until well blended. Stir in the chocolate morsels and pecans.

3. Turn the mixture into the prepared pastry shell. Bake for about 40 to 45 minutes, or until a thin crust forms on top and a wooden pick inserted in the center comes out clean.

4. Remove the pie from the oven, and cool on a rack until the pie just barely reaches room temperature. This will take from 3 to 4 hours. If the pie is cut and served too soon, the filling will be unpleasantly soft.

5. To serve, dust the top generously with confectioners' sugar put through a wire sieve, cut the pie into wedges, and serve with Derby Whipped Cream alongside.

MAKES 8 SERVINGS.

Derby Whipped Cream

1 cup heavy cream
1/4 cup sifted confectioners' sugar
1 tablespoon bourbon

Using a wire whisk or electric beaters, whip the cream with the sugar and bourbon just until it mounds slightly. Turn into a serving bowl, and use immediately; or refrigerate, and use within an hour or two. If held longer, the cream may separate.

NEWPORT CUSTARD PIE WITH CHOCOLATE GLAZE

The title tells it all, except that Newport is a small town in Vermont near the Canadian border, and the custard is flavored with vanilla and almond extracts, not nutmeg.

> 1 unbaked 8-inch Flaky Pastry Shell (page 196)
> 3 large eggs, at room temperature
> 1/2 cup sugar
> 1/4 teaspoon salt
> 1/2 teaspoon vanilla extract
> 1/4 teaspoon almond extract
> 2 cups milk
> Chocolate Glaze (recipe follows)

1. Prepare the pastry shell, giving it a high, fluted edge, as directed. Set aside. Preheat the oven to 425 degrees, setting a rack in the center.

2. In a large mixing bowl beat the eggs slightly just long enough to blend the yolks and whites thoroughly. Remove about a teaspoon of the mixture, and brush the bottom and sides of the pastry shell; refrigerate while preparing the filling (this will help prevent a soggy crust).

3. Stir the sugar, salt, and vanilla and almond extracts into the remaining beaten eggs.

4. In a small saucepan over medium heat, heat the milk just until bubbles appear around the edge. Gradually blend into the egg mixture; blend well, but do not beat.

5. Strain the custard mixture into the chilled pastry shell. (To avoid any spills, add the last cup of filling to the shell after placing it on the oven rack.)

6. Bake the pie for about 25 minutes, or until the filling is set; it will quiver when the pan is lightly shaken. To test, insert a knife halfway between the outside and center of the cus-

tard. If the filling is done, the knife will come out clean, not milky-looking. Remove from the oven, and cool on a rack.

7. When the pie has cooled but is still barely lukewarm, prepare the chocolate glaze, and spread it evenly over the filling. Let stand until the glaze is firm. Cut the pie into wedges, and serve at room temperature.

Note: Any leftovers should be refrigerated.

MAKES 6 SERVINGS.

CHOCOLATE GLAZE

3 ounces semisweet chocolate, chopped into coarse pieces
2 tablespoons milk

Melt the chocolate with the milk in a small, heavy saucepan set over very low heat. Stir until the chocolate is melted and the mixture is smooth and glossy. Immediately dribble it over the pie filling; then spread evenly.

CHOCOLATE CHIFFON PIE

Ever so airy and rich in chocolate flavor.

A 9-inch baked Flaky Pastry Shell (page 196)
1 envelope unflavored gelatin
1/4 cup cold water
2 ounces unsweetened chocolate, chopped into coarse pieces
1/2 cup hot water
4 eggs, separated, at room temperature
1 cup sugar
1/4 teaspoon salt
1 teaspoon vanilla extract
1/2 cup heavy cream, for garnish
2 tablespoons semisweet chocolate shavings, for garnish
  (page 12)

1. Prepare the pastry shell, using a high, fluted edge, as directed. Bake and cool completely.

2. Sprinkle the gelatin over the cold water, and set aside to soften.

3. Combine the chocolate and hot water in a small, heavy saucepan. Set over low heat, and stir occasionally until the chocolate has melted and the mixture thickens and is smooth. Remove from the heat, and add the softened gelatin; stir until dissolved. Set aside.

4. Using a wire whisk, beat the egg yolks with 1/2 cup of the sugar until creamy. Stir into the chocolate mixture. Return the pan to low heat, and cook, stirring, just long enough to dissolve the sugar completely. Remove from the heat, and blend in the salt and vanilla. Strain into a large mixing bowl.

5. Beat the egg whites until soft peaks form; then gradually beat in the remaining 1/2 cup sugar, a tablespoon at a

time. Continue beating until a stiff meringue forms and the sugar has dissolved. Fold into the gelatin mixture.

6. Pour into the baked piecrust, and refrigerate until set. When ready to serve, whip the cream, and spread it over the top of the pie filling. Garnish with the shaved chocolate.

MAKES 8 TO 10 SERVINGS.

COCOA ALMOND PARTY PIE

Toasted almonds and chocolate whipped cream in a pastry shell. What pie could be easier?

A baked 9-inch Flaky Pastry Shell (page 196)
3/4 cup blanched slivered almonds
1 1/2 teaspoons unflavored gelatin
1/4 cup cold water
1/2 cup unsweetened cocoa powder
1 cup confectioners' sugar
2 cups heavy cream
2 teaspoons vanilla extract
Chocolate Lace (page 12)

1. Prepare the pastry shell as directed. Bake and cool. Toast the almonds as directed on page 20; cool. Then scatter them over the bottom of the pastry shell.

2. Sprinkle the gelatin over the water, which has been poured into a small mixing bowl; set aside for 5 minutes to soften. Place the bowl over a small saucepan partially filled with hot water, set over low heat and stir until the gelatin is dissolved. Remove from the heat to cool.

3. Put the cocoa and sugar through a wire sieve into the large bowl of an electric mixer. Gradually stir in first the cream, then the vanilla. Beat until light and fluffy. Gradually beat in the dissolved gelatin. When the mixture forms stiff peaks, turn into the baked pastry shell. Refrigerate for several hours to set before serving.

4. When the filling has set, melt the chocolate for the lace garnish, using 1 ounce semisweet and 1/2 ounce unsweetened chocolate. Drizzle over the top of the filling; chill until the lace is set, about 5 minutes, or until ready to serve.

MAKES 6 TO 8 SERVINGS.

PINK PEPPERMINT PIE WITH CHOCOLATE ICING

The use of melted peppermints in the filling and a chocolate glaze sets this pie apart from the realm of other gelatin pies.

> 1 baked 9-inch Flaky Pastry Shell (page 196)
> 1/2 cup (4 ounces) hard peppermint candies*
> 1 envelope unflavored gelatin
> 1 1/2 cups half-and-half cream or milk
> 2 egg yolks, at room temperature
> 3 egg whites, at room temperature
> 1/8 teaspoon salt
> 6 tablespoons sugar
> 1/2 cup heavy cream
> Chocolate Icing (recipe follows)
> Crushed peppermint candies, for optional garnish

1. Prepare and bake the pastry shell as directed. It should have a high, fluted edge to hold the filling and frosting.

2. Pulverize the 1/2 cup peppermint candies in a blender or a food processor; they need not be turned into powder, simply turned into small enough pieces to melt easily. Set aside.

3. Sprinkle the gelatin over 1/4 cup of the half-and-half cream; stir, and set aside to soften. (It will not soften as well as when water is used.)

4. Beat the egg yolks slightly in a medium-size saucepan. Gradually stir in the remaining 1 1/4 cups cream. Cook over low heat, stirring constantly, until the mixture coats a clean metal spoon. (Do not allow the mixture to boil, or it will curdle.)

5. Remove the custard from the heat, and add the gelatin and crushed candies. Stir until both are completely dissolved.

---

*The peppermint candies used are those hard round and flat ones with red and white stripes, which are usually available in supermarkets.

Refrigerate, stirring occasionally, until the mixture begins to thicken and barely holds a shape.

6. In a large mixing bowl beat the egg whites with the salt until very soft peaks form. Then gradually beat in the sugar, and continue beating until they are stiff. Fold in the candy mixture.

7. Whip the cream until it mounds slightly, and fold it into the custard mixture. Spoon the filling into the prepared pastry shell, shaking the pan gently to smooth the filling. Chill for several hours until firm.

8. Prepare the chocolate icing, and spread it immediately over the pie filling. Refrigerate again until ready to serve.

9. To serve, remove the pie to room temperature, and let it stand until the icing softens just long enough so that it can be easily cut through without breaking. As an optional garnish, sprinkle the edge of the pie with additional crushed peppermint candies.

MAKES 6 TO 8 SERVINGS.

CHOCOLATE ICING

1/3 cup unsalted butter, softened
1/3 cup sifted confectioners' sugar
1 egg yolk
1 1/2 ounces unsweetened chocolate
1/2 teaspoon vanilla extract

Cream together the butter, sugar, and egg yolk. Melt the chocolate in a small saucepan. When it is melted and stirred until smooth, add the butter mixture along with the vanilla; stir until smooth and creamy (do not beat). Use immediately.

BRANDY ALEXANDER PIE

The same combination of ingredients—cognac, cream, and crème de cacao—required for a brandy Alexander cocktail makes a delicious pie.

Chocolate Crumb Crust (recipe follows)
1 1/2 teaspoons unflavored gelatin
1/3 cup water
1/4 cup sugar
1/4 teaspoon salt
4 egg yolks, at room temperature
1/4 cup cognac
1/4 cup crème de cacao, a chocolate-flavored liqueur
1 cup heavy cream

1. Prepare the crumb crust, reserving the crumbs required for garnish. Refrigerate while preparing the filling.

2. Sprinkle the gelatin over the water in a medium-size, heavy saucepan. When it is softened, about 5 minutes, stir in the sugar, salt, and egg yolks. Set over low heat, and cook, stirring, until the gelatin dissolves and the mixture thickens slightly. Do not allow it to come to a boil. Remove from the heat, and let cool for several minutes.

3. Slowly stir the brandy and liqueur into the slightly cooled custard mixture; if they are added rapidly, the sauce may curdle. Pour into a shallow bowl, and refrigerate until the mixture is cool but not jelled.

4. Whip the cream until it holds a definite shape. Fold into the thickened mixture, blending evenly. Turn into the chilled crumb crust. The mixture will be thin compared to other gelatin pies. Sprinkle the reserved cookie crumbs over the top as a simple garnish. Refrigerate, but let stand at room temperature for about 20 minutes before serving, for best flavor.

MAKES 6 SERVINGS.

CHOCOLATE CRUMB CRUST

1 1/2 cups chocolate wafer crumbs
1/4 cup sugar
1/4 cup (1/2 stick) unsalted butter, melted

Combine the cookie crumbs, sugar, and melted butter. Reserve 1 tablespoon for garnish. Press the remainder firmly and evenly onto the bottom and sides (just to the rim) of a well-greased 9-inch pie plate. Chill.

IX

SPECIALTY PASTRIES

CRÊPES AU CHOCOLAT
LACY CRÊPES WITH CHOCOLATE GLAZE
MEXICAN CHOCOLATE TORTILLAS
BITTERSWEET CHOCOLATE ORANGE PUFFS
BOUCHÉES RENÉ
BEIGNETS WITH CHOCOLATE AND APRICOT
SAUCES
CHOCOLATE MERINGUE COFFEE CAKE

CRÊPES AU CHOCOLAT

Tender lacy crêpes rolled with a chocolate butter filling. The crêpes are heated just long enough so that the filling becomes meltingly soft. A hot orange marmalade sauce with walnuts provides the finishing touch.

8 Lacy Crêpes (recipe follows)

CHOCOLATE FILLING

2 ounces semisweet chocolate, chopped into coarse pieces
1/2 cup (1 stick) unsalted butter
1/2 cup sugar
1 large egg, at room temperature
1 egg yolk, at room temperature

MARMALADE TOPPING AND GARNISH

1/2 cup orange marmalade
1 tablespoon Grand Marnier or other orange-flavored liqueur
1/4 cup chopped walnuts

1. Prepare the crêpes in advance, and store as directed. Bring to room temperature before separating them.
2. *For the filling:* Cook the chocolate and butter in a small saucepan set over very low heat, stirring until melted and blended. Add the sugar, and blend until dissolved; cool to lukewarm. Add the egg and egg yolk; beat until creamy. Set the pan in a bowl filled with ice cubes and water; beat until the mixture is stiff, like frosting (this will take only a few minutes).

Fill each crêpe with a heaping spoonful (about 1 1/2 tablespoons) of the filling, placing it down the center; fold one side over, and tuck under the filling; then continue to roll up. Place the seam side down on a narrow serving platter. Continue filling the crêpes, and line them up on the platter in one long row. Cover the platter with plastic wrap, and refrigerate until ready to serve, several hours or overnight if desired.

3. *For the topping:* Combine the orange marmalade and Grand Marnier in a small saucepan. Cover and set aside until ready to use.

4. To serve, bring the covered crêpes to room temperature. Place uncovered in a preheated 250-degree oven just long enough to soften the filling slightly, only a few minutes. (It should be almost to the melting point but not completely melted.) While the crêpes are warming, heat the marmalade mixture until thin and hot (if it is not pourable, add a few drops of the orange liqueur).

5. Remove the platter of crêpes from the oven. Then spoon the hot marmalade over the top. Garnish with the chopped walnuts, sprinkling them over evenly. Serve immediately.

MAKES 8 SERVINGS.

LACY CRÊPES

2 medium-size eggs, at room temperature
6 tablespoons unsifted all-purpose flour
1/4 cup milk
1/4 cup water
1/8 teaspoon salt
1 tablespoon brandy
1 tablespoon unsalted butter, melted
About 2 tablespoons unsalted butter, for cooking the crêpes

1. These crêpes are made in an electric blender. Drop the eggs into the container; then add, in order, the flour, milk,

water, salt, brandy, and melted butter. Blend on low speed for a few seconds, or just until smooth. Cover the container, and refrigerate for at least 2 hours, overnight if preferred.

2. Heat a 6 1/2-inch crêpe pan (measured across the bottom) or a heavy iron skillet over medium-high heat (it is ready when a drop or two of water skids across the pan). Then immediately lift the pan off the heat, and add about 1/2 teaspoon of the butter; rotate the pan to cover the bottom evenly. Return the pan to the heat, and pour in 2 tablespoons of the batter (a standard 1-ounce coffee measure is perfect). Quickly tilt and rotate the pan to cover the bottom evenly. Ideally the batter should barely coat the bottom, even letting some holes remain.

Note: If the pan is too hot, the batter will sputter and pop; if not hot enough, the crêpes will look gummy. The perfect crêpe is one that is delicately browned, tender, thin, and lacy. If the first crêpe seems too thick, thin the batter with a little water.

3. Cook the batter over medium heat for about 18 to 20 seconds, or until the edges are faintly browned. Lift the edge with a small spatula; with your fingers quickly flip it over, and cook it for another 10 seconds. (This second side will be a spotty brown.) Tilt the pan, and turn out the crêpe, spotty side up, onto a sheet of foil large enough to hold and wrap all the crêpes.

4. Repeat the cooking procedure with the remaining batter, buttering the pan lightly before making each crêpe. Stack them evenly on the foil as they are prepared; cool the crêpes; then wrap and refrigerate them until ready to use, up to 1 week. If desired, the crêpes may be frozen; they will keep well up to 1 month. Bring to room temperature, wrapped, before separating, to avoid tearing.

MAKES 10 TO 12 CRÊPES.

LACY CRÊPES WITH CHOCOLATE GLAZE

A special dessert: The crêpes are folded into quarters, topped with grated chocolate, sugar, and butter, then baked until the chocolate has melted and the edges of the crêpes are crisp.

> *10 Lacy Crêpes (page 220)*
> *2 ounces semisweet chocolate, grated (page 9)*
> *1 1/2 teaspoons granulated sugar*
> *2 tablespoons unsalted butter, melted*
> *Confectioners' sugar, for garnish*

1. Prepare and store the crêpes in advance as directed. Bring to room temperature before separating.

2. Preheat the oven to 350 degrees, setting a rack in the center. Generously grease a round 10- to 12-inch heatproof serving plate.

3. Fold each crêpe in half, then in half again to form a triangle. Arrange in a single layer on the prepared plate, over-lapping them slightly (rounded sides toward the edge) and placing one in the center.

4. Sprinkle the tops of the crêpes with first the grated chocolate, then the granulated sugar. Drizzle the melted butter over the top.

Note: If desired, cover and refrigerate, but bring to room temperature before baking.

5. Cover the plate loosely with foil (mounded slightly so that it does not touch the tops of the crêpes). Bake for about 20 minutes, or until the crêpes are hot, the chocolate has melted, and the edges of the crêpes are slightly crisp.

6. Dust the tops of the crêpes with confectioners' sugar, put through a wire sieve, and serve immediately.

MAKES 5 SERVINGS.

MEXICAN CHOCOLATE TORTILLAS

A unique multilayered but thin torte made with flour tortillas and chocolate sour cream filling. The dessert is simple, with only three basic ingredients. The hardest part of making it will be locating a store which sells the tortillas.

> *6 ounces semisweet chocolate, chopped into coarse pieces*
> *1 1/4 cups cold dairy sour cream*
> *1 teaspoon ground cinnamon*
> *1 teaspoon vanilla extract*
> *7 6- to 6 1/2-inch-in-diameter flour tortillas**
> *1 tablespoon confectioners' sugar*
> *Chocolate shavings (page 12), for garnish*

1. In the top of a small double boiler combine the chocolate, 1 cup of the sour cream, and the cinnamon. Set the pan over simmering water, and stir until the chocolate is melted and blended with the sour cream. Remove from the heat; then stir in the vanilla, and set aside, stirring occasionally until firm enough to spread, less than 10 minutes. (To hurry the process, place the pan in a bowl of cold water.)

2. Have ready a flat serving plate. Holding one of the tortillas in your hand, spread the top with one-sixth of the frosting (a generous 1/4 cup) to the edges. Place this tortilla on the serving plate; then repeat the procedure with the remaining tortillas, ending with an unfrosted one on the top. Press down gently; set aside.

3. Combine the remaining 1/4 cup of the sour cream with the confectioners' sugar; blend until smooth. Spread evenly over the top (not the sides) of the stacked tortillas. Cover with an

---

*Flour tortillas are paper-thin wafers made with wheat flour, not with corn flour, as are those which are more familar (do not substitute). They are available fresh or frozen in all stores that carry Mexican products and in some supermarkets. If they are frozen, defrost and dry them, if necessary, before using.

inverted bowl that is large enough so that it touches neither the top nor the sides. Then refrigerate for at least 8 hours before serving, so that the tortillas and chocolate frosting seem to meld together.

4. When ready to serve, garnish the top of the torte with the shaved chocolate.

MAKES 8 SERVINGS.

BITTERSWEET CHOCOLATE ORANGE PUFFS

A classic cream puff accented with the zest of an orange, topped with chopped almonds, and filled with orange-flavored chocolate whipped cream.

> *1/2 cup water*
> *4 tablespoons unsalted butter, cut into slices*
> *1/8 teaspoon salt*
> *1 tablespoon grated rind from 1 orange*
> *1/2 cup sifted all-purpose flour*
> *2 large eggs, at room temperature*
> *1 egg yolk, at room temperature, slightly beaten with*
> *   1 teaspoon water*
> *1/4 cup blanched, fine-chopped almonds*
> *Bittersweet Cream Filling (recipe follows)*

1. Preheat the oven to 450 degrees.
2. Combine the water, butter, salt, and orange rind in a small, heavy saucepan; bring to a rolling boil over medium heat. Add the flour all at once; turn the heat to low, and beat briskly with a wooden spoon until the mixture leaves the sides of the pan.
3. Remove the pan from the heat, and beat in the eggs, one at a time (do not add the second egg until the first has been completely incorporated). Cool slightly for easier handling.
4. Drop the mixture by tablespoonfuls onto an ungreased cookie sheet, spacing them about 3 inches apart. Brush the tops lightly with the beaten egg yolk; then sprinkle the tops with the almonds.
5. Bake the pastries for 15 minutes; then reduce the heat to 350 degrees, and bake for 15 minutes longer, or until well puffed and golden brown. The tops should feel crisp and dry. Remove from the oven, and immediately remove with a spatula to cooling racks to cool slightly. While they are still warm,

slice off the top third of each puff, using a serrated knife, and lay them on the racks. Allow the puffs to cool completely before filling.

6. When ready to serve, prepare the filling. Use a teaspoon to fill the pastries; then cover each with its own top.

Note: The unfilled pastries, once cooled, may be held for several hours at room temperature without losing their crisp quality. If desired, they may be baked a day in advance but must be reheated in a 200-degree oven for about 8 minutes, or until crisp and firm. Cool before using.

MAKES 12 PUFFS.

BITTERSWEET CREAM FILLING

6 ounces semisweet chocolate, chopped into coarse pieces
3 tablespoons fresh orange juice
1 cup heavy cream

1. Melt the chocolate with the orange juice in the top of a double boiler set over barely simmering water. Stir until blended and smooth; then cool for about 10 minutes.

2. In a chilled bowl, with chilled beaters, whip the cream until it holds firm peaks. Gradually fold in the melted chocolate mixture, blending carefully until it is one color. Use immediately.

Note: Once filled, the puffs will hold up well for about an hour at a cool room temperature; do not refrigerate.

BOUCHÉES RENÉ

These tartlets are made of cream puff pastry and filled with an exceptionally rich and shiny chocolate sauce, which firms as it cools. They would go well with demitasse or could accompany a scoop of vanilla ice cream served as dessert.

2/3 cup water
1/8 teaspoon salt
6 tablespoons (3/4 stick) unsalted butter, cut into slices
3 tablespoons sugar
2 teaspoons grated orange rind (zest only)
2/3 cup sifted all-purpose flour
2 large eggs, at room temperature
Chocolate Filling (recipe follows)

1. Lightly grease thirty-six miniature (1 3/4 inch in diameter, measured across the top) muffin cups. Set aside.

2. Combine the water, salt, butter, sugar, and orange rind in a small, heavy saucepan. Place over medium heat, and bring to a rolling boil, at which point the butter should be melted. Reduce the heat to simmer; add the flour, and stir briskly with a wooden spoon until the mixture comes away from the sides of the pan.

3. Remove the pan from the heat, and beat in the eggs, one at a time, making sure that the first egg is well incorporated before adding the second; then continue to beat until smooth and shiny. Let stand for 20 minutes or so, until the dough can be handled.

4. Form the dough into 1-inch balls, and place in the muffin tins. Make a deep indentation in the center of each with your finger; then work the dough evenly up the sides to the rim (it should be perhaps the thickest here).

5. Preheat the oven to 400 degrees, setting two racks one just above and one just below the center. Place the muffin tins

in the oven, and immediately reduce the heat to 375 degrees. Bake for 23 to 25 minutes, or until the rims of the pastry are barely golden brown. (You may need to reverse and turn the pans toward the end for even browning.) Remove from the pans immediately, and cool on wire racks. Use within an hour or two to preserve the crispness.

Note: The pastry shells may be frozen. To use, place the frozen shells individually on a baking sheet; bake in a hot oven just long enough to crisp them slightly. Cool before filling.

6. No more than a few hours before serving, prepare the chocolate filling. Spoon into the tartlets, filling them almost to the rim. Let stand at room temperature until set. (Although the filling stays creamy and moist, the filled pastry shells lose their tender crispness as the hours advance.)

Note: The bouchées are served without garnish, but their appearance is enhanced when they are served in small fluted paper liners.

MAKES 36 BOUCHÉES.

CHOCOLATE FILLING

6 ounces semisweet chocolate, chopped into coarse pieces
6 tablespoons sugar
6 tablespoons heavy cream
3 tablespoons unsalted butter
3/4 teaspoon vanilla extract

Melt the chocolate, sugar, and cream in the top of a small double boiler set over hot, but not boiling, water. When the mixture is smooth, add the butter and vanilla. Continue cooking, stirring frequently, for about 5 minutes, or until the mixture is shiny and thickens slightly. Remove from the heat, and use immediately.

BEIGNETS WITH CHOCOLATE AND APRICOT SAUCES

Beignets are crisply fried French fritters, delicately crusty on the outside, tender within. These sweet fritters are served piping hot and are accompanied by two quickly made complementary sauces, one bittersweet chocolaty, the other made with apricot preserves.

> *3/4 cup water*
> *6 tablespoons unsalted butter, cut into slices*
> *1 tablespoon granulated sugar*
> *1/8 teaspoon salt*
> *3/4 cup sifted all-purpose flour*
> *3 large eggs, at room temperature*
> *Vegetable oil, for shallow frying*
> *Confectioners' sugar, for garnish*
> *Bittersweet Chocolate Sauce (recipe follows)*
> *Apricot Sauce (recipe follows)*

1. Pour the water into a small, heavy saucepan, and add the butter, granulated sugar, and salt. Bring to a rolling boil, at which point the butter should be melted. Add the flour all at once. Lower the heat, and cook, stirring constantly with a wooden spoon, for a minute or two, until the mixture comes away from the sides of the pan.

2. Remove the pan from the heat, and beat in the eggs, one at a time, incorporating each egg thoroughly before adding the next. Continue beating until thick and smooth. Allow the mixture to cool while heating the oil.

3. Pour enough vegetable oil in a large skillet so that it is at least 1 inch deep. Heat to 360 degrees.

4. Drop the mixture by heaping teaspoonfuls into the hot oil, frying only a few beignets at one time so that they are not crowded. Fry for about 4 to 5 minutes, or until they are crusty

and a dark golden brown, turning occasionally with a spoon so that they color evenly.

Note: It is important that the fritters are crusty; if under-cooked, they will deflate before being served. Using a 10-inch skillet, you should be able to fry 10 fritters at a time (one-third the mixture).

5. When they are sufficiently cooked, remove the fritters with a slotted spoon, and drain on paper toweling. Place successive batches in a 250-degree oven to keep hot while frying the remainder.

6. Place the beignets on a heated serving platter, and dust the tops generously with confectioners' sugar put through a wire sieve. Pass the sauces separately.

MAKES ABOUT 30 BEIGNETS OR 6 SERVINGS.

BITTERSWEET CHOCOLATE SAUCE

4 ounces semisweet chocolate
1 ounce unsweetened chocolate
1/2 cup water
2 1/2 tablespoons unsalted butter
1/2 cup confectioners' sugar

Chop the chocolates into coarse pieces, and place in the top of a double boiler set over barely simmering water. Add the water, butter, and sugar. Stir occasionally until the chocolate is melted and the mixture is well blended and smooth. Remove from the heat, but keep the sauce over hot water until ready to serve. It should be served warm.

APRICOT SAUCE

1 cup apricot preserves
3 to 4 tablespoons apricot brandy or water

Turn the apricot preserves into a small saucepan. Add 3 tablespoons of the brandy or water, and simmer, stirring, just until thoroughly heated. Add additional liquid, if necessary, to bring to a sauce consistency. Serve warm.

Note: If there are any large pieces of fruit in the preserves, break them up while heating.

CHOCOLATE MERINGUE COFFEE CAKE

A wonderful yeast-risen coffee cake with a swirl of chocolate and nut meringue in the center. Unlike most yeast breads, this one rises overnight in the refrigerator.

YEAST DOUGH

1 cup (2 sticks) unsalted butter
1/2 cup milk
2 1/2 cups sifted all-purpose flour
2 tablespoons granulated sugar
1/4 teaspoon salt
2 packages dry yeast
1/4 cup warm (110-degree) water
3 egg yolks, at room temperature

CHOCOLATE MERINGUE FILLING

3/4 cup plus 6 tablespoons granulated sugar
2 teaspoons ground cinnamon
3/4 cup semisweet chocolate morsels
3/4 cup chopped walnuts
3 egg whites, at room temperature
Confectioners' sugar, for garnish

1. *For the yeast dough:* Melt the butter with the milk in a saucepan; allow to cool until lukewarm.

Sift the flour with the 2 tablespoons granulated sugar and salt; set aside.

Sprinkle the yeast over the warm water in a measuring

cup; stir to dissolve. Pour into a large mixing bowl. Add the egg yolks, one at a time, and stir until blended. Blend in the butter and milk mixture. Then gradually add the flour mixture; mix well. Turn the dough into a greased bowl; turn to bring the greased side up. Cover the bowl with plastic wrap, and refrigerate overnight or for at least 12 hours.

When the dough has chilled properly, grease well a 10-inch tube pan with a removable bottom. Preheat the oven to 350 degrees, setting a rack one-third up from the bottom.

2. *For the meringue filling:* Mix 6 tablespoons of the granulated sugar and cinnamon; set aside. Combine the chocolate morsels and walnuts; set aside.

In a large mixing bowl whip the egg whites until soft peaks form; then gradually beat in the remaining 3/4 cup granulated sugar. Continue beating until the mixture forms a glossy meringue. Set this aside briefly while rolling out the yeast dough.

3. Divide the chilled dough into two parts. Place one portion on a floured board, and roll into a 12 × 9-inch rectangle. Spread half the meringue mixture over the dough to within 1/4 inch of the edges. Sprinkle with half the cinnamon mixture, then half the chocolate-nut mixture to cover the meringue evenly.

4. Roll up the dough loosely as for a jelly roll, beginning at the wide end. Moisten the edges of the dough with water; pinch edges together to seal well. Transfer, seam side down, into the prepared pan (it will fill half). Repeat the procedure with the remaining dough and filling. Moisten the ends, and pinch together.

5. Bake for 1 hour, or until the top is crisp and golden brown. Cool for 10 minutes on a rack; then loosen and remove the outside rim, leaving the bottom and center tube intact. Cool completely; then remove the coffee cake, carefully lifting it from the tube, placing your hands at the sides where the dough was joined. (Or cut a few slices first; this makes removal from the pan easier.) Dust liberally with confectioners' sugar before serving.

Note: This coffee cake is particularly delectable when served slightly warm. Bake and cool; then reheat in a warm oven, dusting with the confectioners' sugar just before serving.

MAKES 12 OR MORE SERVINGS.

X

COOKIES

SEVEN-MINUTE FUDGIES
DOUBLE CHOCOLATE DROP COOKIES
SAUCEPAN CHOCOLATE CRINKLES
FAVORITE FUDGE BROWNIES
CHOCOLATE SHERRY CREAM BARS
CHOCOLATE MINT SPLIT SECONDS
PEANUT BUTTER PINWHEELS
PEANUT BUTTER NUGGETS
SUMMER COOKIES
SPICED CHOCOLATE COOKIES
CINNAMON COCOA SHORTBREAD
CAPPUCCINOS
CHOCOLATE BUTTER PECAN BARS
CHOCOLATE THINS
SCANDINAVIAN CHOCOLATE WAFERS
CHOCOLATE DÉLICES

SEVEN-MINUTE FUDGIES

The ultimate in chewy, fudgy cookies.

> 2 cups (12 ounces) semisweet chocolate morsels
> 1/4 cup (1/2 stick) unsalted butter
> 1 14-ounce can sweetened condensed milk
> 1 teaspoon vanilla extract
> 1 cup sifted all-purpose flour
> 1 cup coarse-chopped pecans

1. Preheat the oven to 350 degrees, placing a rack in the center. Have ready three ungreased cookie sheets. (The cookie dough should be placed on the sheets while warm but should be baked individually for accurate timing.)

2. Combine the chocolate morsels, butter, and milk in a large, heavy saucepan (it will serve as a mixing bowl). Set over medium heat and stir frequently until the chocolate and butter are melted and combined smoothly with the milk. Remove from the heat; cool slightly; then stir in the vanilla. Add the flour and pecans, stirring just until well mixed.

3. Drop the warm mixture by teaspoonfuls in small mounds on the cookie sheets, spacing them about 1 1/2 inches apart.

4. Bake each filled cookie sheet individually for about 7 minutes. (The cookies will appear underbaked but will firm once cooled.) Remove the cookie sheet to a wire rack, and let stand just until the cookies are set enough to be removed easily with a spatula. Place on wax paper (set on a flat surface) until completely cooled.

Note: These cookies must be served within a few hours after baking for perfect moist and chewy quality. Leftovers seem to dry, even though stored in an airtight container.

MAKES 4 1/2 TO 5 DOZEN COOKIES.

DOUBLE CHOCOLATE DROP COOKIES

Soft cakelike cookies with a delicious chocolate glaze and a garnish of chopped pistachios.

> 2 cups sifted all-purpose flour
> 1/2 teaspoon baking powder
> 1/4 teaspoon baking soda
> 1/4 teaspoon salt
> 1/2 cup (1 stick) unsalted butter, softened
> 3/4 cup packed light brown sugar
> 1 egg, at room temperature
> 1 teaspoon vanilla extract
> 3 ounces unsweetened chocolate, melted
> 2/3 cup milk
> Chocolate Frosting (recipe follows)
> 1/2 cup chopped pistachios, for garnish

1. Preheat the oven to 350 degrees.

2. Sift together the flour, baking powder, baking soda, and salt; set aside.

3. In a large bowl, with an electric mixer at medium speed, cream the butter with the sugar. Add the egg and vanilla; beat until light and fluffy. Blend in the melted chocolate.

4. Beat in alternately the sifted flour mixture and milk, beginning and ending with the flour mixture.

5. Drop the mixture by heaping tablespoonfuls, about 2 inches apart, onto greased baking sheets. Bake for about 10 minutes, or just until firm when pressed with a finger. Remove to a wire rack to cool.

6. Prepare the chocolate frosting. Use to frost the tops of the cookies generously; then sprinkle with the chopped pistachios.

MAKES ABOUT 30 COOKIES.

CHOCOLATE FROSTING

1 1/2 cups semisweet chocolate morsels
3 tablespoons unsalted butter
1/3 cup milk
3 cups sifted confectioners' sugar
1 1/2 teaspoons vanilla extract

Place the chocolate morsels, butter, and milk in the top of a double boiler set over barely simmering water. Stir until the chocolate is melted and the mixture is smooth. Remove from the heat, and beat in the sugar and vanilla. Use at once to frost the cookies.

SAUCEPAN CHOCOLATE CRINKLES

A soft and chewy cookie, when properly made, with a baked-on garnish of powdered sugar.

1 ounce unsweetened chocolate, chopped into coarse pieces
2 tablespoons unsalted butter
1/2 cup superfine sugar
1/2 cup sifted all-purpose flour
1/2 teaspoon baking powder
1/8 teaspoon salt
1 egg, at room temperature
1/2 teaspoon vanilla extract
1/2 cup coarse-chopped pecans
Confectioners' sugar

1. Place the chocolate and butter in a 1 1/2-quart saucepan or one large enough in which to mix the cookie dough. Melt over low heat. Remove from the heat; stir to blend; then stir in the superfine sugar. Set aside to cool slightly.

2. Sift together the flour, baking powder, and salt; set aside.

3. Beat the egg and vanilla in a mixing bowl with a fork until frothy. Gradually stir into the cooled chocolate mixture. Add the flour mixture and blend; then stir in the pecans. Cover and set aside the saucepan, so that the dough cools to room temperature, about 1 hour, and is no longer sticky.

4. Preheat the oven to 350 degrees, and grease a large cookie sheet.

5. Pinch off small portions of the dough, and shape into balls by rolling between the palms of the hands. They should be about 1 inch in size. Roll each one as it is formed into the confectioners' sugar to cover; then place an inch apart on the cookie sheet.

6. Bake for 7 to 8 minutes, or just until a wooden pick

barely comes out clean. The cookies will appear soft and under-baked, but do not bake further or they will not be chewy. Let them cool just long enough on the cookie sheet to remove; then lift them off with a spatula, and cool on wire racks. (The dough will crack unevenly as the cookies bake; this is characteristic of a cookie of this type.)

7. When the cookies are thoroughly cooled, store them in a covered container to preserve the soft texture.

MAKES ABOUT 24 COOKIES.

FAVORITE FUDGE BROWNIES

An old-time recipe but one of the best.

2 eggs, at room temperature
1 cup granulated sugar
1/2 cup (1 stick) unsalted butter
2 ounces unsweetened chocolate, chopped into coarse pieces
3/4 cup sifted all-purpose flour
1/2 teaspoon salt
1 cup pecan halves
1 teaspoon vanilla extract
Confectioners' sugar, for garnish

1. Preheat the oven to 325 degrees. Grease well an 8-inch square baking pan.

2. Beat the eggs slightly; blend in the granulated sugar.

3. Melt the butter with the chocolate in a small, heavy saucepan set over very low heat. Blend into the butter mixture. Add the flour, salt, pecans, and vanilla; stir until well blended (do not beat).

4. Turn the mixture into the prepared baking pan. Bake for 30 to 35 minutes, or until a toothpick inserted in the center comes out clean but not dry. Do not overbake; the brownies should be soft and slightly moist when served.

5. Cool in the pan set on a rack. Then sprinkle the top with confectioners' sugar, and cut into squares. Or cut into finger strips, and roll in confectioners' sugar for dainty dessert cookies.

MAKES 16 SQUARES OR 32 FINGERS.

CHOCOLATE SHERRY CREAM BARS

This is a fudgy brownie type of bar with two toppings: one creamy and white and flavored with sherry; the other a thin glaze of nearly pure chocolate. The bars are best served when well chilled, even frozen.

> 1 cup (2 sticks) unsalted butter
> 4 ounces unsweetened chocolate
> 4 eggs, at room temperature
> 1/2 teaspoon salt
> 2 cups sugar
> 1 cup sifted all-purpose flour
> 1 teaspoon vanilla extract
> Sherry Cream Topping (recipe follows)
> Chocolate Glaze (recipe follows)

1. Generously grease a 15 1/2 × 10 1/2 × 1-inch jelly roll pan. Preheat the oven to 325 degrees.

2. Melt the butter and chocolate together in a heavy saucepan set over low heat. Stir occasionally to blend evenly. Remove from the heat, and set aside to cool slightly.

3. In the large bowl of an electric mixer beat the eggs with the salt until foamy. Slowly add the sugar while beating; continue beating just until the mixture is creamy. Add the chocolate mixture, flour, and vanilla. Beat just until smooth.

4. Pour the batter into the prepared pan, tipping it slightly to cover the bottom evenly. Tap the pan two or three times on the counter to eliminate excessive air bubbles. Bake for 25 minutes, or until a pick inserted in the center comes out clean. Cool in the pan on a wire rack.

5. When the cake has cooled to room temperature, prepare the sherry topping. Spread it evenly over the top. Refrigerate for about 1 hour, or until the topping is firm and cold.

6. Prepare the chocolate glaze. While it is hot, drizzle it over the topping; then quickly spread it evenly, using the back

of a teaspoon. Refrigerate until the glaze is set; then cover the pan securely with foil. Return the pan to the refrigerator or freezer. Do not attempt to cut into bars until the glaze has hardened.

7. To serve, cut into 2-inch squares; then serve cold or partially frozen.

MAKES 40 BARS.

SHERRY CREAM TOPPING

1/2 cup (1 stick) unsalted butter, softened
4 cups (1 pound) confectioners' sugar, sifted
1/4 cup light or heavy cream
1/4 cup dry sherry
1 cup coarse-chopped walnuts (optional)

Cream the butter in a mixing bowl until light. Gradually beat in the sugar alternately with the cream and sherry. When smooth, stir in the walnuts, if used. Use immediately.

CHOCOLATE GLAZE

1 cup (6 ounces) semisweet chocolate morsels
4 tablespoons (1/2 stick) unsalted butter
3 tablespoons water

Melt the chocolate morsels with the butter and water in a small saucepan set over low heat. Blend well, remove from the heat, and cool for a minute or two, but use while hot.

CHOCOLATE MINT SPLIT SECONDS

Rich and tender chocolate cookies with a minty green filling. The dough is baked in two long rolls with a depression in the center to receive the filling. They are sliced diagonally, then served so that the original shape of the roll is retained.

1 1/2 cups unsifted all-purpose flour
1/2 teaspoon baking soda
1/4 teaspoon salt
1 1/4 ounces unsweetened chocolate, chopped into coarse
   pieces
1/2 cup (1 stick) unsalted butter, softened
1/2 teaspoon vanilla extract
6 tablespoons sugar
1 small egg, at room temperature
1 tablespoon water
Creamy Mint Frosting (recipe follows)
Chocolate sprinkles (page 13), for garnish

1. Sift together the flour, baking soda, and salt; set aside. Melt the chocolate, and set aside to cool.

2. In a mixer bowl cream the butter; add the vanilla and sugar, and beat just to mix well. Add the egg and water; beat until blended. Then blend in the melted chocolate. Add the sifted dry ingredients in thirds, mixing on low speed only until well mixed. Scrape the dough into a mound onto a sheet of wax paper; wrap and refrigerate for at least 1 hour, or until firm, or for several hours, if desired.

3. When ready to bake the cookies, preheat the oven to 350 degrees, setting a rack in the center. Lightly grease a large cookie sheet.

4. Divide the chilled dough into two parts. Roll each portion separately on a lightly floured board to form long narrow rolls about 1 inch in diameter and about 13 inches long. Trans-

fer the rolls to the cookie sheet. Pat each to flatten slightly; then make a depression about 1/3 inch deep lengthwise down the center of each with a knife handle.

5. Bake the rolls for 10 minutes; remove from the oven, and increase the depression, using the back of a measuring teaspoon (tap it gently, rather than draw it down the center). Return the pan to oven, and continue baking for about 5 minutes longer, or until the rolls are firm to a light touch.

6. Place the cookie sheet on a rack, and allow to cool for 10 minutes while preparing the frosting. Spoon the frosting into the depressions, and sprinkle the tops lightly with chocolate sprinkles. Let stand just until the frosting is set and firm; then cut diagonally into bars about 3/4 inch wide.

Note: Although the cookies may be separated and served individually, for a special presentation carefully remove the sliced bars with a long spatula to a serving platter or board, retaining the original shape of the roll.

MAKES 30 TO 32 COOKIES.

CREAMY MINT FROSTING

2 tablespoons unsalted butter
1 tablespoon milk
1 cup confectioners' sugar, sifted
1/2 teaspoon peppermint extract
A few drops green food coloring (optional)

Melt the butter in a small saucepan. Remove from the heat; add the milk, sugar, and peppermint. Beat until smooth and creamy; then blend in a drop or two of the food coloring, just enough to tint the frosting a pale green.

PEANUT BUTTER PINWHEELS

Like old-fashioned, and fondly remembered, peanut butter cookies with a swirl of chocolate in the center of each.

> 1/2 cup vegetable shortening
> 1 cup sugar
> 1/2 cup creamy-style peanut butter
> 1 egg, at room temperature
> 1 tablespoon milk
> 1 1/2 cups sifted all-purpose flour
> 1/2 teaspoon salt
> 1/2 teaspoon baking soda
> 1 cup (6 ounces) semisweet chocolate morsels

1. Cream the shortening, sugar, and peanut butter until light. Mix by hand with a wooden spoon. Beat in the egg and milk. Sift together the flour, salt, and baking soda; stir into the creamed mixture. Then work together with your hands to form a dough. Form roughly into a long and flat rectangle.

2. Place the dough on a sheet of lightly floured wax paper. Place a clean sheet of wax paper over the top. Roll out with a rolling pin into a 15 × 8-inch rectangle. Remove the top sheet of paper, and trim the edges of the dough.

3. Melt the chocolate morsels in the top of a double boiler set over hot water; stir until smooth, and cool slightly. With a small spatula spread the chocolate evenly over the rolled dough to the edges.

4. Starting at the widest edge, roll up the dough firmly like a jelly roll, lifting the paper slightly with each turn. Wrap, seam side down, in the wax paper, and refrigerate on a cookie sheet for 30 minutes, just long enough to firm the chocolate.

5. Preheat the oven to 375 degrees.

6. Roll the chilled dough back and forth in its wrapping to return to a cylindrical form because it will have flattened on

the bottom. Cut across into 1/4-inch slices with a sharp knife (don't expect perfect rounds), and place 1 inch apart on ungreased baking sheets. Bake for about 10 to 12 minutes, or until lightly golden. Remove immediately to wire racks for cooling.

MAKES 5 DOZEN LARGE COOKIES.

PEANUT BUTTER NUGGETS

A simple cookie made with three ingredients and an even easier frosting made from milk chocolate bars. If you like commercial peanut butter cups, you will cherish this recipe.

> *1 cup creamy-style peanut butter*
> *1 cup sugar*
> *1 large egg, at room temperature*
> *2 1/2 bars (about 1 1/2 ounces each) milk chocolate**
> *Chopped toasted peanuts, for optional garnish*

1. Preheat the oven to 350 degrees. Lightly grease a large cookie sheet.

2. Combine the peanut butter, sugar, and egg in a large mixing bowl, mixing with a wooden spoon until well blended. Let stand for 10 minutes.

3. Form the dough into 1-inch balls, and place 1 to 1 1/2 inches apart on the cookie sheet. Bake for about 10 minutes, or until barely golden. (Watch carefully because the bottoms tend to brown rapidly.)

4. While the cookies are baking, break the chocolate bars into sections. As the cookies come from the oven, place a piece of chocolate on the top of each. Return the pan to the oven just long enough to soften the chocolate, less than 30 seconds.

5. Spread the melting chocolate over the tops of the cookies; then sprinkle a few chopped peanuts, if desired, in the center of each. Remove the cookies to racks for cooling.

MAKES 30 COOKIES.

*Plain milk chocolate Hershey bars are required.

SUMMER COOKIES

An unbaked confection made with chocolate, peanut butter, and oatmeal. Couldn't be easier, couldn't be better.

2 cups sugar
4 tablespoons unsweetened cocoa powder
1/2 cup (1 stick) unsalted butter, cut into chunks
1/2 cup milk
1/2 cup creamy-style peanut butter
3 cups uncooked quick rolled oats
1 teaspoon vanilla extract

1. Have ready two large cookie sheets lined with wax paper.

2. Combine the sugar and cocoa in a 2-quart heavy saucepan; mash any lumps. Add the butter and milk. Cook over medium heat, stirring, just until the sugar dissolves. Allow the mixture to come to a full boil. Immediately remove from the heat, and add the peanut butter, oats, and vanilla. Mix well; then drop the mixture by teaspoonfuls in rounded mounds onto the wax paper. Set aside until set.

MAKES ABOUT 40 COOKIES.

SPICED CHOCOLATE COOKIES

A butterless cookie that contains minute particles of pecans and bitter chocolate and is spiced with cinnamon and cloves. The cookies are slightly chewy when properly stored.

2 large eggs, at room temperature
1 cup granulated sugar
Scant 1/4 teaspoon salt
2 cups pecans, chopped into very fine pieces
2 ounces unsweetened chocolate, grated (page 9)
1 ounce semisweet chocolate, grated (page 9)
1/4 cup fine dry breadcrumbs
2 tablespoons flour
1 teaspoon ground cinnamon
1/4 teaspoon ground cloves
Confectioners' sugar, for garnish

1. In a large mixer bowl, with electric beaters, beat the eggs slightly; then gradually beat in the sugar and salt. Continue beating on medium speed for about 5 minutes, or until the mixture is thick and creamy and forms a quickly dissolving ribbon when the beaters are lifted. Remove from the beaters.

2. Stir in the pecans and grated chocolates. Combine the breadcrumbs, flour, cinnamon, and cloves; mix well. Then add to the pecan mixture, and mix in thoroughly. Scrape down the sides, cover the bowl, and refrigerate for at least 1 hour, or until the dough can be handled.

3. Preheat the oven to 350 degrees. Then form the dough into 1 1/4-inch balls between the palms of your hands; it will be sticky. Roll in the confectioners' sugar lightly, but cover completely. Place on well-greased cookie sheets at least 1 inch apart.

4. Bake the cookies for about 15 minutes, or until they have crackled and are barely firm to the touch. Remove from the cookie sheets, and cool on wire racks. Store airtight when they are completely cooled. (They keep well for weeks.)

MAKES 4 DOZEN COOKIES.

CINNAMON COCOA SHORTBREAD

A crisp buttery cookie that is easily made. The dough is pressed into a cake pan for baking, then cut into wedges for serving.

1 1/2 cups sifted all-purpose flour
1/2 cup sifted cake flour
1/4 cup sifted unsweetened cocoa powder
3/4 cup confectioners' sugar
1/2 teaspoon ground cinnamon
1 cup (2 sticks) cold unsalted butter
1 tablespoon granulated sugar, mixed with 1/8 teaspoon
   cinnamon

1. Preheat the oven to 350 degrees. Have ready two ungreased 8-inch round layer cake pans.

2. Combine both flours, the cocoa, confectioners' sugar, and cinnamon in a large mixing bowl. Slice the butter into the flour mixture. Mix with your fingertips to make coarse crumbs Then work the dough until smooth and well blended by kneading with your hands.

3. Divide the dough in half, and press evenly into the cake pans. Sprinkle the tops with the sugar and cinnamon mixture. Prick the entire surface with the tines of a fork (as you would for a pastry shell).

4. Bake the shortbreads for about 25 minutes, or until they are firm to the touch. Cool on racks for 10 minutes; then cut each shortbread into 16 wedges. Allow to cool completely before removing. To store, leave the shortbreads in the pans, and cover tightly with foil. They will stay crisp for days.

MAKES 32 THIN WEDGES.

CAPPUCCINOS

Devastatingly rich chocolate chip bars that are flavored with espresso and brushed with a thin cinnamon glaze. These cookies are crisp and keep well.

1 cup (2 sticks) unsalted butter, softened
1 cup firm-packed light brown sugar
1 tablespoon powdered (not granular) instant espresso coffee
1 teaspoon vanilla extract
2 1/4 cups sifted all-purpose flour
1/2 teaspoon baking powder
1/2 teaspoon salt
2 cups (12 ounces) semisweet chocolate morsels
Cappuccino Glaze (recipe follows)

1. Preheat the oven to 350 degrees. Have ready a greased 15 1/2 × 10 1/2 × 1-inch jelly roll pan.

2. Using an electric mixer, cream the butter, sugar, espresso, and vanilla until light and fluffy. Sift the flour with the baking powder and salt; blend into the butter mixture. Remove from the mixer, and stir in the chocolate morsels.

3. Press the dough evenly onto the bottom of the pan, using your fingers. Bake for about 25 minutes, or until golden brown. Set aside on a rack while preparing the glaze.

4. Prepare the glaze, and brush it evenly over the top of the warm cappuccinos. Just before it sets and while the cappuccinos are still warm, cut into 2-inch bars. When completely cool, cover the pan with foil for storing.

MAKES 40 BARS.

CAPPUCCINO GLAZE

1 tablespoon butter
1/4 teaspoon ground cinnamon
3/4 cup confectioners' sugar, sifted
About 2 tablespoons milk

Melt the butter with the cinnamon in a small saucepan set over very low heat. Remove from the heat, and alternately add the sugar and milk, using enough milk to make a thin glaze. Use immediately.

CHOCOLATE BUTTER PECAN BARS

So rich and buttery that one small piece should satisfy anyone's sweet tooth. The bars are topped with milk chocolate morsels.

CRUST

2 cups sifted all-purpose flour
1 cup packed light brown sugar
1/2 cup (1 stick) unsalted butter, slightly softened

FILLING AND TOPPING

1 cup pecan halves
2/3 cup (1 1/3 sticks) unsalted butter
1/2 cup packed light brown sugar
1 cup (6 ounces) milk chocolate morsels

1. Lightly grease a 13 × 9-inch baking pan. Preheat the oven to 350 degrees, setting a rack in the center.

2. *For the crust:* Combine the flour and the 1 cup sugar in a mixing bowl. Cut the stick of butter into chunks, and add. Using a pastry blender, cut in the butter until it is well blended and small crumbs are formed. Turn the mixture into the baking pan, and press it evenly and firmly over the bottom.

3. *For the filling and topping:* Arrange the pecans, rounded sides up, over the pastry; press in lightly. Combine the 2/3 cup butter and 1/2 cup sugar in a 1 1/2-quart saucepan. Place over moderate heat, and stir until the sugar and butter are melted and the mixture comes to a full boil. Spoon over the pastry

base. (There is enough to cover it thinly and completely.) Sprinkle the chocolate morsels evenly over the top.

4. Bake the mixture for 18 to 20 minutes, or until the sides are bubbling. Do not overbake; the center will cook through upon cooling. Remove the pan, and set on a rack to cool.

5. When the pan feels almost cold to the touch, loosen the sides with a thin sharp knife. Cut into small squares, about 1 1/4 to 1 1/2 inch in size. Cover the pan tightly with foil until ready to serve.

MAKES ABOUT 6 DOZEN SQUARES.

CHOCOLATE THINS

Wafer-thin cookies, rich and delicious. A bit exacting to make, but the results are worth the effort.

1/2 cup (1 stick) unsalted butter
2 ounces unsweetened chocolate, chopped into coarse pieces
1 1/2 cups granulated sugar
1 large egg, at room temperature
1/2 teaspoon vanilla extract
1/2 cup sifted all-purpose flour
1/2 teaspoon baking powder
1/4 teaspoon salt
6 large red candied cherries, cut into sixths
Confectioners' sugar, for garnish

1. Preheat the oven to 325 degrees, setting a rack in the center.

2. Combine the butter and chocolate in a medium-size, heavy saucepan; it will serve as a mixing bowl. Melt over very low heat, stirring until smooth. Remove from the heat, and stir in the granulated sugar; then blend in the egg and vanilla.

3. Sift the flour with the baking powder and salt; blend into the chocolate mixture. Cool slightly.

4. Drop the chocolate mixture by slightly rounded measuring teaspoonfuls onto a greased cookie sheet, spacing them 2 inches apart. Place a piece of candied cherry in the center of each. (One standard sheet will accommodate 12 cookies, and each sheet should be baked separately.) Bake each sheet for 10 to 12 minutes. The mixture will spread out thinly and bubble; do not remove from the oven until the bubbling has stopped, or the wafers will be underbaked and cannot be removed from the sheet as directed.

Note: You may want to bake two or three cookies as a test for proper baking.

5. Remove the cookie sheet from the oven, and allow the wafers to stand for a few minutes until set; then remove with a spatula to racks for cooling.

6. Store at a cool room temperature in a tightly covered container with wax paper between the layers.

7. When ready to serve, dust half of each wafer top with confectioners' sugar put through a wire sieve. (This garnish as well as the use of the candied cherries is optional but makes an attractive presentation.)

MAKES 36 3 1/2-INCH WAFERS.

SCANDINAVIAN CHOCOLATE WAFERS

Pale chocolate-flecked cookies with a slightly bitter overtone. They are rolled thin and cut into rounds for baking, then sandwiched together with currant jelly.

> 1/3 cup unsalted butter, softened
> 2 hard-cooked egg yolks, sieved*
> 1/4 cup granulated sugar
> 1 teaspoon vanilla extract
> 1 cup sifted all-purpose flour
> 1/2 cup semisweet chocolate morsels, grated (page 9)
> Red currant jelly, for filling
> Confectioners' sugar, for garnish

1. Preheat the oven to 400 degrees.

2. Place the butter, egg yolks, granulated sugar, and vanilla in a mixing bowl. Blend well with a wooden spoon. Stir in the flour and grated chocolate; blend well to form a dough by kneading with your hands. Chill briefly if it is too soft to roll.

3. Roll out half the dough at one time between sheets of wax paper to slightly less than 1/4-inch thickness. Cut into 2-inch rounds with a cookie cutter. Place an inch apart on ungreased cookie sheets. (Scraps may be rerolled.)

4. Bake the cookies for about 8 minutes, or until the bottoms are delicately browned. (Test one to determine.) Cool the cookies on racks.

5. When ready to serve, melt a few tablespoons of the currant jelly to thin; spread over half the cookies, and top with the remainder. Dust the tops with confectioners' sugar.

MAKES 12 TO 14 DOUBLE COOKIES.

*The yolks of hard-cooked whole eggs may be used. To cook the yolks alone, carefully separate the yolks from raw eggs without breaking the yolks. One by one, place in a spoon, and lower into simmering water; simmer for 10 minutes, or until cooked through; cool. (The whites may be stored in a screw-top jar in the refrigerator for a week or so or may be frozen.)

CHOCOLATE DÉLICES

A crisp almond butter cookie with a simple chocolate filling and optional garnish. The basic cookie may also be served plain. See the notation at the end of the recipe.

1 1/2 cups sifted all-purpose flour
3/4 cup fine-ground blanched almonds, toasted (page 20)
3/4 cup (1 1/2 sticks) cold unsalted butter
1/2 cup granulated sugar
Chocolate Filling (recipe follows)
Confectioners' sugar and candied red cherries, or sliced
   unblanched almonds, for garnish

1. Preheat the oven to 350 degrees. Have ready one or two ungreased cookie sheets and a roll of wax paper. You will also need 1 1/2-inch and 3/4-inch round cookie cutters (or a thimble).

2. Combine the flour and ground almonds in a mixing bowl (the almonds must be ground almost to the powdery state, so that the cookie cutters will cut the edges of the dough neatly). Cut the cold butter into thin slices from the bar directly into the flour mixture; then work with your fingertips to make very coarse crumbs. Add the sugar. Then work the dough until smooth and well blended by kneading with your hands. Divide the dough into two parts, and refrigerate half while rolling out the other.

3. Roll the dough between sheets of wax paper to slightly less than 1/8-inch thickness. Remove the top layer of paper. Then cut the dough into 1 1/2-inch rounds, and transfer to an ungreased cookie sheet, placing them less than 1 inch apart. (For a sheet that measures 15 × 12 inches, you will be able to accommodate 30 cookies—5 across and 6 rows down.) Cut out the centers of half the cookies, using a 3/4-inch round cutter or thimble. Remove and place the centers with the dough trimmings; set aside for subsequent rolling and cutting. (Since no

additional flour is used for rolling, these scraps when rerolled will be as good as the first cookies made.)

4. Bake the cookies, one sheet at a time, for 8 to 10 minutes, or until they are set and barely turn color from white to golden. (At 8 minutes they may seem pale; watch carefully for the next minute or two because they will turn color rapidly.)

5. When the cookies are perfectly baked, remove the sheet, and let stand for a minute or two to set; then remove the cookies with a spatula to racks to cool completely.

6. When all the cookies are baked and cooled, prepare the chocolate filling. Spread the bottoms of the solid cookies thinly with the melted chocolate; then cover with the cutout cookies, bottom sides down, and press them lightly together. Sift confectioners' sugar lightly over the tops; then either press a tiny bit of candied cherry in the center of each to give them a little color or insert a slivered almond or two.

7. When the filling is set, store the cookies between sheets of wax paper in a tightly covered container. Or freeze.

Note: These cookies, without filling, are ideal to be served along with any dessert (chocolate or other) for which a simple butter cookie seems appropriate. The rings alone are attractive when dusted with confectioners' sugar, but the plain cookie rounds when formed with a scalloped cookie cutter are a better choice and as appealing in appearance—and take less time to prepare.

MAKES 4 TO 4 1/2 DOZEN FILLED COOKIES.

CHOCOLATE FILLING

4 ounces semisweet chocolate, chopped into coarse pieces
1 tablespoon unsalted butter

Partially melt the chocolate and the butter in a small, heavy saucepan set over direct heat. Remove from the heat and stir rapidly until the mixture is smooth and has a spreading consistency. (If it is slightly stiff, stir in a minute amount more butter to bring it to the proper consistency.) Use immediately.

XI

CONFECTIONS

ORANGE CHOCOLATE CHIP MERINGUES
MACADAMIA COCOA MERINGUES
BEACON HILL COOKIES
MINIATURE FRENCH CHOCOLATE CAKES
FRENCH CHOCOLATE TRUFFLES
SARAH BERNHARDTS
FROZEN MINT FRANGOS
CHOCOLATE ALMOND LACE
COCONUT LACE WAFERS
CHOCOLATE FRAGMENTS
BUTTER ALMOND CRUNCH
CHOCOLATE CHUNKIES
GLACÉED CHERRY ALMOND CHOCOLATES
CHOCOLATE ALMONDS

ORANGE CHOCOLATE CHIP MERINGUES

Sugary sweet and best served with demitasse cups of black espresso.

>   3 large-egg whites, at room temperature
>   Scant 1/4 teaspoon salt
>   1/4 teaspoon cream of tartar
>   1 cup sugar
>   1/2 teaspoon vanilla extract
>   1/4 teaspoon almond extract
>   1 tablespoon grated rind from 1 orange
>   1 cup (6 ounces) semisweet chocolate morsels

1. Preheat the oven to 300 degrees. Have ready two ungreased baking sheets.

2. In the small bowl of an electric mixer beat the egg whites until foamy. Add the salt and cream of tartar; continue to beat at medium speed until soft peaks form. Gradually add the sugar, a tablespoon at a time. When all the sugar has been added, add the vanilla and almond extracts. Continue beating at high speed until the meringue is very stiff and the sugar is dissolved.

3. Using a rubber spatula, fold in the grated orange rind and the chocolate morsels, mixing thoroughly.

4. Drop the mixture by heaping teaspoonfuls onto the cookie sheets. Bake for 25 minutes, or until the tops feel crisp and dry to the touch.

5. Remove the cookie sheets from the oven, and allow the meringues to cool on them. Carefully remove with a wide spatula.

Note: The meringues may be stored in an airtight container for at least two weeks.

MAKES ABOUT 3 1/2 DOZEN.

MACADAMIA COCOA MERINGUES

Crunchy and crisp and put together like sandwiches. The macadamia nuts dominate the taste and provide interesting texture.

1/2 cup granulated sugar
2 tablespoons unsweetened cocoa powder
2 large-egg whites, at room temperature
1/8 teaspoon salt
1/8 teaspoon cream of tartar
1/2 teaspoon vanilla extract
2/3 cup macadamia nuts*
Chocolate Filling (recipe follows)
Confectioners' sugar, for garnish

1. Preheat the oven to 275 degrees, setting two racks, one just above and one just below the center. Have ready two ungreased, large baking sheets.

2. Put the granulated sugar and cocoa through a wire sieve into a small bowl; stir to blend completely. Set aside.

3. In the small bowl of an electric mixer beat the egg whites until foamy. Add the salt and cream of tartar; continue to beat until the egg whites are stiff but not dry, adding the vanilla toward the end of the beating.

4. Remove the egg whites from the mixer; then fold in the cocoa and sugar mixture in four or five additions, sprinkling each over the top but not blending completely before the next. With the last addition the mixture should be completely blended. Fold in the macadamia nuts.

5. Drop the mixture by heaping teaspoonfuls onto the baking sheets 1 1/2 to 2 inches apart. (You should be able to

---

*Macadamia nuts are a Hawaiian product sold in most grocery stores in cans or jars. There is a mix of whole and half nuts; cut any whole nuts into halves before using.

drop 16 mounds on each sheet, so that all the meringues are baked at one time.)

6. Bake the meringues for about 30 minutes, or until they feel dry to the touch and the bottoms are completely baked and glazed. (Test one meringue after 25 minutes of baking to determine.) Immediately remove with a spatula, and allow to cool on racks or the counter.

7. When the meringues have cooled, prepare the chocolate filling. Spread half the meringue bottoms thinly with the filling (using just enough to "glue" them together); then top with the remainder, selecting two of comparable size. Allow the meringues to stand at room temperature until the filling is firm before serving.

8. For an attractive presentation, pile the meringues in a silver serving bowl or glass compote. Then dust the tops lightly with confectioners' sugar.

Note: The filled meringues keep well stored in an airtight container.

MAKES 16 DOUBLE-FILLED MERINGUES.

CHOCOLATE FILLING

1 ounce semisweet chocolate, chopped into coarse pieces
1 tablespoon butter

Melt the chocolate and butter in a very small saucepan. As soon as they are melted and blended, the filling is ready to use.

BEACON HILL COOKIES

A meringue type of confection made with melted chocolate and walnuts.

> 1 cup (6 ounces) semisweet chocolate morsels
> 2 egg whites, at room temperature
> 1/2 cup sugar
> 1/2 teaspoon white vinegar
> 1/2 teaspoon vanilla extract
> 3/4 cup chopped walnuts

1. Preheat the oven to 350 degrees.

2. Melt the chocolate morsels, stirring, in the top of a double boiler set over hot water; set aside to cool until barely warm.

3. Beat the egg whites until soft peaks form. Gradually add the sugar, a tablespoon at a time, and continue beating until the whites form stiff peaks. Add the vinegar and vanilla toward the end of the beating.

4. Fold in the melted chocolate and walnuts; blend lightly but evenly.

5. Drop by small teaspoonfuls onto a greased cookie sheet. (Space the mixture 2 inches apart to allow for spreading.) Bake for 10 minutes. (They will be crisp on the outside, moist within.) Cool the cookies on the baking sheet.

MAKES ABOUT 5 DOZEN.

MINIATURE FRENCH CHOCOLATE CAKES

Chocolate-glazed gems—deliciously moist, incredibly rich.

>   6 tablespoons unsalted butter, softened
>   1/2 cup sugar
>   3 large eggs, separated, at room temperature
>   2 tablespoons flour
>   4 ounces unsweetened chocolate, melted and cooled
>   1/8 teaspoon salt
>   Chocolate Glaze (recipe follows)

1. Generously grease twenty-four miniature (measuring 1 3/4 inches across the top) muffin cups. Preheat the oven to 325 degrees, setting a rack in the center. Have ready a baking sheet on which to place the pans.

2. Place the 6 tablespoons softened butter in a mixing bowl. Using a wire whisk, whip until smooth. Gradually blend in the sugar; then add the egg yolks, one at a time, whisking until the mixture is well blended and slightly thickened. Fold in the flour; then stir in the melted chocolate.

3. Beat the egg whites with the salt until stiff but still moist. Stir about one-third into the chocolate mixture until blended; fold in the remainder.

4. Spoon into the prepared muffin tins. The batter is stiff and the indentations will be heaping; it is not necessary to level the batter because it settles in baking.

5. Place one of the filled pans on the baking sheet. Bake in the preheated oven for about 6 to 8 minutes. The edges should feel slightly firm, the centers dry but soft. Do not over-bake; the centers will firm as the cakes cool. Remove from the baking sheet, and cool in the pans. Repeat the process with the second pan.

6. When the cakes are cool, remove from the pans, and set, inverted, on a sheet of wax paper placed on a flat surface.

7. While the cakes are cooling, prepare the chocolate glaze. When it has cooled to the proper consistency for dipping (not quite spreadable), dip each cake individually into the glaze, turning it to coat completely. As each is dipped, invert and place it on the wax paper. Let the cakes stand until the glaze has set and the bottoms can be easily peeled away from the paper. (The tops and sides will firm up before the bases; do not attempt to remove before the glaze is set.)

8. Store the coated cakes at room temperature. Since they are completely sealed by the glaze, these confections may be made several days in advance.

MAKES 24 MINIATURE CAKES.

CHOCOLATE GLAZE

3 ounces semisweet chocolate, chopped into coarse pieces
1 teaspoon unsalted butter
3 tablespoons Grand Marnier or other orange-flavored
  liqueur

Melt the chocolate with the butter in a small saucepan set in a small skillet of simmering water. Remove from the heat, and stir in the Grand Marnier. Let stand until it has a proper consistency for dipping. To hurry the process, set the pan in a bowl of ice water, and stir constantly.

FRENCH CHOCOLATE TRUFFLES

A classic French sweet, often served in tiny fluted paper cups.

1 cup (2 sticks) unsalted butter
8 ounces semisweet chocolate, chopped into coarse pieces
1/2 cup brandy
Unsweetened cocoa powder

1. Cut the butter into pieces directly into a heavy saucepan. Melt over medium-low heat; then turn heat to medium, and when the butter bubbles, stir to mix well. When the bubbling turns to foam, remove from the heat.

2. Let stand for 5 minutes to settle; then skim any remaining foam from the top. Carefully pour off the clear liquid, leaving the light brown sediment in the saucepan. Wipe it clean with paper toweling.

3. Return the butter (this is called clarified butter) to the clean saucepan. Add the chopped chocolate. Stir over very low heat until the chocolate is melted and smoothly blended with the butter. Remove the pan from the heat, and cool slightly. Stir in the brandy. Refrigerate for several hours, or until the mixture is firm enough to handle, or overnight. (Stir the mixture occasionally as it begins to chill to prevent the butter from separating and rising to the top.)

4. Shape the chilled mixture into irregular, lumpish balls to resemble truffles, about 1 to 1 1/4 inches in diameter.

5. Sprinkle the cocoa on a sheet of wax paper, and roll the truffles in it to coat. Place in a single layer in a pan, and refrigerate until firm. Then store between sheets of wax paper in a tightly covered container in the refrigerator. The truffles will keep well for several weeks. Serve chilled.

MAKES 3 TO 3 1/2 DOZEN TRUFFLES.

SARAH BERNHARDTS

A remarkable taste experience: half almond macaroon and half creamy chocolate truffle with a thin chocolate coating. These confections are said to have been invented in Denmark in the late 1800s as a tribute to the French actress.

1/4 cup (1/2 stick) unsalted butter, softened
1 1/2 cups confectioners' sugar, sifted
2 ounces unsweetened chocolate, chopped into coarse pieces
1 1/2 teaspoons instant espresso powder
2 tablespoons amaretto, an almond-flavored liqueur
1/8 teaspoon salt
24 amaretti (Italian macaroons)*
Chocolate Glaze (recipe follows)

1. In a small bowl mix the butter with the sugar, using a fork. They will not blend together completely, but mix them long enough to form tiny particles. Set aside.

2. Place the chocolate in a small saucepan; sprinkle the espresso over the top, and add the amaretto and salt. Melt over very low heat, stirring, until the mixture is smooth. Immediately add to the butter, and mix with a fork until the two mixtures are well blended and smooth. Let stand or chill until the mixture is firm enough to handle.

3. Roll the chocolate mixture by hand into small balls, about 1 inch in diameter. There should be 24. Press each one onto the flat side of one of the amaretti cookies, molding and rounding it so that it covers the bottom completely. (You will have a cookie that is well rounded—half amaretti, half truffle.) Complete the process with the remaining cookies and truffle

---

*Amaretti are very crisp almond macaroons. The brand required is Amaretti di Saronno, Lazzaroni & Co., which is available in Italian stores and gourmet food sections of department stores. They are sold in 16-ounce tins (or larger), with the 1 1/2-inch macaroons wrapped two together in pastel tissue paper.

mixture. Let stand at room temperature for about 30 minutes, or until set.

4. Prepare the chocolate glaze. One by one, dip the truffle side of the prepared confections into the melted chocolate, covering it completely but leaving the macaroon unglazed. Set aside, glazed sides up, on a wire rack set over a tray to cool.

5. When the glaze has set, the Sarah Bernhardts may be served. To store, wrap them individually in the amaretti papers, and place in a covered container. Refrigerate, but bring to room temperature before serving. They will keep well for weeks.

MAKES 24.

CHOCOLATE GLAZE

4 ounces semisweet chocolate, chopped into coarse pieces
1 tablespoon vegetable oil (not butter or margarine)

Combine the chocolate and oil in the top of a small double boiler, and set it over barely simmering water. (Or use a small mixing bowl set over a saucepan.) Melt the chocolate, stirring constantly, until it is smooth and satiny. (The stirring "tempers" the chocolate and ensures good color and quicker hardening after the macaroons have been dipped.) Immediately remove the pan from the water; overcooking will turn the chocolate gray and dull when hard. Use immediately.

FROZEN MINT FRANGOS

A delightful minty and pale chocolaty confection molded in miniature paper cups. Perfect to serve with coffee after dinner.

1 cup (2 sticks) unsalted butter, softened
1 teaspoon vanilla extract
3/4 teaspoon peppermint extract
2 cups confectioners' sugar
4 large eggs, at room temperature
2 ounces unsweetened chocolate, melted and cooled
1/2 cup fine-chopped pecans
Chocolate sprinkles (page 13) and candied cherries, for
    garnish, and fresh mint leaves, for optional garnish

1. Line miniature (1 3/4 inches measured across the top) muffin cups with paper liners, preferably foil. You will need 36. Set aside.

2. In a large mixing bowl and with electric beaters, cream the butter with the vanilla and peppermint extracts until light. Press the sugar through a wire sieve into the butter, and continue to beat until creamy. Add the cooled melted chocolate, and beat until well blended.

3. Beat in the eggs, one at a time, beating on medium speed after each addition until thoroughly blended. After the last egg has been added, beat for at least 2 minutes longer. Fold in the pecans.

4. Spoon the mixture into the paper liners so that they are slightly heaping; then spread to the edges with a knife so that the filling is level at the top. (You may want to reserve a little of the mixture before filling all the liners in order to ensure that each one contains the proper amount.) Garnish the tops lightly with chocolate sprinkles and a tiny piece of candied cherry set in the center.

5. Freeze in the pans until ready to serve, at least 2 hours. Top each frango with a small mint leaf, an optional but attractive garnish when fresh mint is available. Serve while frozen.

MAKES 36 MINIATURE CONFECTIONS.

CHOCOLATE ALMOND LACE

Thin, crisp, and lacy.

4 tablespoons (1/2 stick) unsalted butter
1/2 cup sugar
2 tablespoons light corn syrup
1/2 teaspoon vanilla extract
6 tablespoons sifted all-purpose flour
1/4 teaspoon salt
1/4 teaspoon baking powder
2 tablespoons milk
1 cup chopped blanched almonds (page 20)
3 ounces semisweet chocolate, chopped into coarse pieces
2 teaspoons vegetable oil

1. Preheat the oven to 325 degrees. Line a cookie sheet with a sheet of foil; do not grease.

2. Cream the butter with the sugar until light. Stir in the corn syrup and vanilla.

3. Sift the flour with the salt and baking powder; add to the creamed mixture alternately with the milk; blend until smooth. Stir in the almonds.

4. Drop by rounded measuring teaspoonfuls onto the cookie sheet, spacing them 3 inches apart to allow for spreading. Bake for 10 minutes, or until the edges are well browned and the wafers are bubbling. Let cool completely; then peel away the foil.

5. Melt the chocolate with the vegetable oil over hot water, stirring constantly until smooth and satiny. Brush or spread the chocolate thinly over the undersides of the wafers. Let stand in a cool place until set. If necessary, refrigerate briefly to firm, but do not store in the refrigerator. Place in a tightly covered container to store, with wax paper between the layers.

MAKES 36 2 1/2-INCH WAFERS.

COCONUT LACE WAFERS

Large crisp wafers put together as doubles with melted chocolate. An attractive and special confection.

1/2 cup sifted all-purpose flour
1/2 cup sweetened flaked coconut
1/4 cup packed dark brown sugar
1/4 cup light corn syrup
1/4 cup (1/2 stick) unsalted butter, cut into chunks
1/2 teaspoon vanilla extract
Chocolate Filling (recipe follows)
4 to 5 large red candied cherries, cut into eighths

1. Preheat the oven to 350 degrees, setting a rack in the center. Line a large cookie sheet with a sheet of foil; do not grease.

2. Combine the flour and coconut; set aside.

3. Combine the sugar, corn syrup, and butter in a medium-size, heavy saucepan. Bring to a boil over medium heat, stirring constantly. Remove from the heat; stir in the coconut mixture; then blend in the vanilla.

4. Drop the mixture onto the cookie sheet by slightly rounded measuring teaspoonfuls 3 inches apart. Bake for 8 to 10 minutes, or until a light golden brown. Cool on the pan for at least 3 to 4 minutes, or until firm and the wafers can be lifted off easily. Place on paper toweling to absorb the excess butter.

Note: You will be able to bake only 12 cookies at a time. Reheat the mixture slightly if necessary between bakings. The mixture will spread into irregular rounds; this is part of the charm.

5. When the wafers are cooled, prepare the chocolate filling. Using a table knife, spread a little of the warm chocolate

over the underside of one wafer; place a second wafer, flat side down, on top. Repeat with the rest of the cookies. Place a small piece of candied cherry on top of each.

Note: Use only enough chocolate to "glue" the cookies together, and it should not come to the edges.

6. Set the filled cookies aside at room temperature until the filling is firm. To store, place in a tightly covered container, with wax paper between the layers.

MAKES 18 DOUBLE 3-INCH COOKIES.

CHOCOLATE FILLING

2 ounces semisweet chocolate, chopped into coarse pieces
1 1/4 teaspoons vegetable oil

Melt the chocolate with the vegetable oil in a small bowl set over hot water, stirring constantly until smooth.

CHOCOLATE FRAGMENTS

Unusual and special. These rich broken pieces of chocolate-covered pastry are best served frozen or very, very cold.

1/2 cup (1 stick) unsalted butter, softened
1/2 cup packed light brown sugar
1 egg yolk, at room temperature
1/2 teaspoon vanilla extract
1 cup sifted all-purpose flour
16 ounces dark sweet chocolate, chopped into coarse pieces
1/2 cup coarse-broken pecans

1. Preheat the oven to 350 degrees, setting a rack in the center. Have ready an ungreased 15 1/2 × 10 1/2 × 1-inch jelly roll pan.

2. Place the butter in a mixing bowl. Add the sugar by pressing it through a wire sieve. Using a rubber spatula, cream the two together. Blend in the egg yolk and vanilla. Gradually add the flour, and mix well until thoroughly blended.

3. Spread the dough onto the bottom of the jelly roll pan as evenly as possible; then use a metal pancake turner to scrape down any dough adhering to the sides. Bake for 15 minutes, or until golden brown, reversing the pan halfway through the baking so that the dough browns evenly. Remove the pan from the oven, and cool for 5 minutes.

4. While the cookie dough is baking, melt the chocolate in the top of a double boiler set over barely simmering water. Remove from the heat when partially melted, and stir until smooth.

5. Spread the warm chocolate evenly over the warm cookie dough; then scatter the pecans over the top. Press them in gently with the pancake turner or with your fingers, so that they are firmly set in the chocolate. Allow to cool to room temperature; then place the pan in the freezer.

6. When the chocolate is frozen, and when ready to serve, remove from the freezer. Break into pieces with the point of a knife. (They will be irregular in shape but should be about 2 inches in diameter.) Serve while frozen.

MAKES ABOUT 4 DOZEN IRREGULAR PIECES.

BUTTER ALMOND CRUNCH

This is toffee candy filled with almonds and covered with milk chocolate.

1 cup (2 sticks) unsalted butter, cut into chunks
1 1/3 cups packed light brown sugar
2/3 cup toasted almonds (page 20), chopped into coarse
  pieces
2 thin (about 1 1/2-ounce) bars milk chocolate
1/2 cup toasted almonds (page 20), chopped into fine pieces

1. Grease well a 13 × 9-inch baking pan.

2. Combine the butter and sugar in a heavy 2-quart saucepan. Place over low heat, and stir constantly until the mixture comes to a boil.

3. Continue cooking the mixture, stirring occasionally, until a small amount dropped in cold water is brittle (290 degrees on a candy thermometer). Remove the pan from the heat, and add the 2/3 cup coarse-chopped almonds; stir just long enough to blend in. Immediately pour the mixture into the greased pan. Let stand until set but still warm.

4. Separate the chocolate bars into sections, and place individually over the top of the warm toffee. As the chocolate softens, spread it evenly with a spatula. Sprinkle evenly with the fine-chopped almonds; press in lightly.

5. Cool the coated toffee in the pan. Break into irregular pieces to serve.

MAKES 1 1/3 POUNDS.

CHOCOLATE CHUNKIES

*Nuggets of chocolate: a candy combining bittersweet chocolate with pea-
nut butter chips and pecans.*

> 2 ounces unsweetened chocolate
> 2 ounces semisweet chocolate
> 1 tablespoon unsalted butter
> 1/3 cup packed dark brown sugar
> 1 large egg, at room temperature
> 1 tablespoon cold water
> 1 teaspoon vanilla extract
> 2 tablespoons all-purpose flour, sifted
> 1 cup (6 ounces) peanut butter chips
> 1 cup coarse-chopped pecans

1. Chop the chocolates into coarse pieces; melt together
with the butter in a 1 1/2-quart heavy saucepan set over very
low heat. Remove the pan from heat, and blend in the sugar

2. Using a fork, beat together the egg, water, and vanilla
until frothy. Stir into the chocolate mixture; then blend in the
flour. Add the peanut butter chips and pecans; mix well (the
mixture will be sticky). Cover the pan, and refrigerate for about
1 hour to 1 hour and 10 minutes (no longer, or the mixture
will harden), or until firm.

3. Preheat the oven to 350 degrees, setting two racks one
just above and one just below the center. Line two large cookie
sheets with foil. Have ready a small bowl of ice water.

4. Dip your fingers into the ice water; then pull off small
portions of the chocolate mixture. Pinch together to form
1-inch nuggets. Place about 1 1/2 inches apart on the lined
cookie sheets as they are formed. Bake for 10 minutes, or until
the tops feel dry to the touch. Place on cooling racks, and allow
to cool completely before removing. Store the confections
tightly covered at room temperature.

MAKES 3 DOZEN.

GLACÉED CHERRY ALMOND CHOCOLATES

A chocolate confection that is easily made and different from any you can buy.

16 *(about 3 ounces) red candied cherries*
6 *ounces semisweet chocolate, chopped into coarse pieces*
2 *ounces unsweetened chocolate, chopped into coarse pieces*
2 *tablespoons unsalted butter*
1 *cup (about 4 ounces) slivered, blanched almonds*

1. Cut the cherries into at least 10 to 12 pieces each; set aside.

2. Melt the chocolates together in a small mixing bowl set over a saucepan of barely simmering water. When they are partially melted, turn off the heat, and continue stirring until the mixture is smooth. Set aside.

3. Melt the butter in a small skillet; add the almonds, and stir over low heat until they are lightly toasted. Immediately stir into the melted chocolate (excess butter included). Then stir in the cherry bits.

4. Drop the warm mixture by heaping teaspoonfuls onto wax paper, which has been placed on a flat surface. Let them stand in a cool place until they are hardened and can be lifted from the paper easily. (This may take several hours.)

5. Store the confections in an airtight container in the refrigerator or freezer until ready to use, but bring to room temperature before uncovering and serving.

MAKES 32 TO 34 CONFECTIONS.

CHOCOLATE ALMONDS

An easily made candy and a special addition to a tray of cookies.

Generous 1/2 cup (3 ounces) sliced, unblanched almonds
1 1/2 tablespoons Grand Marnier or other orange-flavored
liqueur
1 cup (6 ounces) semisweet chocolate morsels
1 tablespoon vegetable shortening

1. Carefully mix the almonds with the Grand Marnier in a small mixing bowl. Cover the bowl, and let stand at room temperature for 24 hours.

2. Spread the almonds out onto a lightly greased shallow baking pan. (One about 6 × 10 inches is ideal, so that almonds may be spread evenly in a thin layer.) Bake in a preheated 350-degree oven, turning them occasionally with a spatula so that they toast evenly. When they are a golden color, 10 to 15 minutes, remove the pan from the oven, and cool.

3. Melt the chocolate morsels and shortening in a 1 1/2-quart saucepan set over very low heat. Stir continuously, and remove from the heat once the chocolate has melted. Immediately add the toasted almonds, and stir until they are evenly coated with the chocolate.

4. Drop the mixture by heaping teaspoonfuls onto a sheet of wax paper, which has been placed on a cookie sheet. (One large cookie sheet will accommodate all; because the mixture will not spread, they can be placed close together.)

5. Allow the confections to stand at a cool room temperature for about 1 1/2 hours, or until set. (When ready, they can be easily lifted from the paper without sticking.)

6. Store in a covered container with wax paper between the layers and at a cool room temperature until ready to serve.

MAKES 20 CONFECTIONS.

INDEX